CW00381398

Prophecies
in
Parallel

The author:-

John Greed obtained a Law degree at the University of Bristol in 1959 and qualified as a solicitor in 1963. In 1962 at 24 years of age he became a born-again Christian by accepting Jesus Christ as his Saviour after hearing the gospel preached at a series of open-air meetings at Speakers' Corner in London's Hyde Park.

From 1970 until his retirement in 2000 he taught Law at the University of the West of England, Bristol (formerly Bristol Polytechnic) and he continued to do so part-time after retiring.

In 1998 he was awarded a Ph.D. degree for his dissertation on his research into Land Law, by the University of Reading.

He has elementary qualifications (and they are indeed elementary!) in French, German, Italian, Latin, Greek, Hebrew, Arabic and Sociolinguistics, and he holds a Certificate in Theological Studies (120 credits) from Trinity Theological College, Bristol.

His wife (whom he met at a conference at a Bible College) is Professor of Inclusive Urban Planning at the University of the West of England.

This book is printed on recycled paper.

Prophecies in Parallel

by

John A. Greed
LL.B., Ph.D., Cert.Ed.

2007

A St. Trillo Publication

ii

first published   January, 2007

© John A. Greed 2007

Published by   *St. Trillo Publications,*   *John A. Greed*
St. Trillo House,
92, Hillside Road,
Redcliffe Bay,
Portishead,
Bristol, England.
BS20 8LJ

Printed by   *The UWE Printing and Stationery Services Centre,*
Unit 104, Farendell Road,
Emerald Park East,
Emerson's Green,
Bristol, England.
BS16 7FF

All rights reserved,
*but in the interests of spreading the message, the author will not normally
object to the copying of all or any parts of this work, as long as not copied for
financial gain.*

*John A. Greed asserts his moral right to be identified as the author of
this work.*

10-digit ISBN 0-948685-12-3
13-digit ISBN 978-0-948685-12-5

Contents

- - - - -

Preface

This book is intended to be both a popular easy-to-read account of end-times prophecies, and a serious contribution to the academic debate on the interpretation of those prophecies.

Is it possible to fulfil both these aims in one book? I believe so. There is a certain art in reducing complex arguments to language which ordinary Christians (as against theologians) can follow, without having such over-simplification that the result is a false view. I hope I have gone some way towards achieving that.

I am grateful to several librarians who have provided me with hard-to-obtain material, and I thank no-one for assistance with typing, having typed and typeset every word of it myself!

My prayer is that I don't mislead anybody.

J.A.G.

- - - - -

What this book is about

This book is about seven years of the future!

Many students of prophecy say that there will be a particular seven-year period which will lead up to the Battle of Armageddon and the Second Coming of Jesus. They believe this because of a prophecy called the "seventy weeks" prophecy, which the angel Gabriel gave to the prophet Daniel. (The prophecy is recorded in Chapter 9 of the *Book of Daniel* in the Old Testament of the Bible.)

In Chapter 24 of *Saint Matthew's Gospel* in the New Testament, Jesus warns that this seven-year period will include "great tribulation".

Saint Paul in some of his letters, and Saint John in his *Book of Revelation* (all in the New Testament) add further details.

This book is an attempt to knit these prophecies together and to give an account and a warning of what will happen, together with some speculation on what *might* happen, in that destined seven-year period.

- - - - -

Chapter 1

Daniel's Timescale

The aim of this book

The aim of this book is to show how the Old Testament and New Testament prophecies fit together to give one single message.

How do the "seven Seals" and "seven Trumpets" in *Revelation*, and the prophecy of "seventy weeks" in *Daniel*, and Jesus' prophecy of "great tribulation" all join together? We shall see.

But first we need a timescale to work on, and that is just what the angel Gabriel gave to an old man named Daniel in the year 538 B.C.

Daniel

Daniel was in exile. As a teenager he had been taken away from Jerusalem to Babylon in 605 B.C. Now he was over eighty years old and had become an important political figure in Babylon, but had never been able to return to his homeland. Jerusalem and its Temple were in ruins—burnt in 586 B.C. by Nebuchadnezzar's army. Exile can make people become assimilated into the nation to which they have been taken. "Forget Jerusalem, old man; forget your homeland; forget your nation's history and its god." But Daniel had not forgotten.

Daniel gets a visitor

Then the angel Gabriel came to Daniel. This occasion *(Dan. 9:24-27)* was the second time Daniel had met Gabriel. After the first time (described in *Dan. 8:16-27)* Daniel had been so appalled by the vision he had seen that he had needed to take several days sick leave, but this time he was less overcome.

Gabriel's message: the seventy "sevens" (or seventy "weeks")

The gist of Gabriel's message on this second visit was, "One day, an order to rebuild Jerusalem will be given, and after sixty-nine 'sevens' from that date, Messiah (or an anointed one) will come and will be cut off. After that, the people of a prince who is going to come will destroy the city. He will enforce a covenant for one 'seven' but in the middle of that period he will stop the sacrifices and will erect an abomination of desolation. And the end will be desolation."

We need to look a bit more closely at this.   When does it start?
What is a "seven"? Who is the prince who is going to come?

Here is the full wording of *Dan. 9:25-27*. We shall need to refer
back to it from time to time.

> 25. ... You are to know and discern that from the issuing of a decree
> to restore and rebuild Jerusalem until Messiah *[or an anointed one]*
> the Prince, there will be seven "sevens" *[or "weeks"]* and sixty-two
> "sevens". It will be rebuilt with streets and a trench *[or moat]* even in
> times of distress.
> 26. After the sixty-two "sevens", Messiah *[or an anointed one]* will
> be cut off and will have nothing. The people of the prince who is to
> come will destroy the city and the sanctuary *[the Temple]*. The end
> will come with a flood; right to the end there will be war; desolations
> have been decreed.
> 27. He will make firm a covenant with the many for one "seven", but
> in the middle of the "seven" he will put a stop to sacrifice and grain
> offering; and on the wing of abominations comes one who makes
> desolate, until a complete destruction, one that is decreed, is poured out
> on the desolator *[or, on a wing or pinnacle of the Temple he will set
> up an abomination that causes desolation, until the end that is decreed
> is poured out on him]*.

But first, why did Gabriel visit Daniel?

Gabriel's arrival

Here is what happened.   Daniel was reading what the prophet
Jeremiah had written, and he came across the prophecy that Jerusalem
would be in ruins for seventy years and then would be rebuilt. (The
prophecy is in *Jer. 25:11-12* and *29:10*.) Daniel prayed: and then, while
he was still praying about the seventy *years*, Gabriel appeared and
announced that he had come to tell Daniel about seventy *sevens* for the
Jews and for Jerusalem *(Dan. 9:2, 16-17, 23-24)*.

In this prophecy, a "seven" (or a "week") means seven years, not
seven days. So "seventy sevens" is 70 x 7 years = 490 years.

The first sixty-nine "sevens"

Gabriel then spoke of seven sevens plus sixty-two sevens (making
sixty-nine sevens: 69 x 7 years = 483 years) starting from the date of an
Order to Rebuild Jerusalem, and he said that after the end of that period,
"Messiah (or an anointed one) shall be cut off and shall have nothing".

And the prophecy came true. In the month that the 483-year period expired, Jesus was crucified and had nothing. (See pages 96-99 for the complicated details of the timing of this.)

That deals with 483 of the 490 years: it leaves us just seven years to look for.

The seventieth "seven" after the "times of the gentiles"

Gabriel told Daniel that there would be a gap between the sixty-ninth and the seventieth seven. Look at *Dan. 9:26-27.* (Warning: this is tricky. Gabriel is deliberately talking in riddles: he only intended this information for those who are willing to sit down and work it out. So take it slowly, step by step.)

As we have just seen on page 2, verse 26 is quite a long one. It begins, "Messiah (or an anointed one) will be cut off and will have nothing"—but then it does *not* go on to the seventieth seven but deals with another event first. It says, "The people of the ruler who will come will destroy the city *[Jerusalem]* and the sanctuary *[the Jerusalem Temple]*". (We'll think about what that means in a minute.) Then it speaks of the end "with a flood", and "war" and "desolations". And *then* in verse 27 Gabriel tells of the last seven:

> **He (i.e. the ruler who will come, that Gabriel mentioned above) will confirm a covenant with many for one seven.**

This prophecy in verse 27 has never been fulfilled, so it refers to a period of history which has not happened yet. But what does it mean? Let's try to work it out by starting at the end and working backwards.

One "seven"

We know that this means seven years. This is our final seven years. (More exactly, it may turn out to be 6 years and 10¾ months, because Gabriel may have worked on 360-day years, as we shall see on page 96: but let's call it seven years, for convenience.)

A covenant with many

A covenant is a promise or an agreement or a treaty—such as a peace treaty. And this entire prophecy is about the Jews and Jerusalem: Gabriel said so, as we saw on page 2 above—so this is a peace treaty to do with Israel (i.e. the Jews) and Jerusalem.

The coming ruler will *confirm* this covenant

The verb is in the *hiphil* (causative) tense: the coming ruler is going to *cause* the treaty to be firm—he's going to *enforce* it.   He will not necessarily be involved in negotiating it—but he will *enforce* it.

But who is this ruler?

Who is he? We don't yet know his name—he hasn't appeared on the pages of history yet—but we know where he will come from.   Look back at verse *26:* "The *people* of this ruler will destroy Jerusalem and the Temple". *That* part of the prophecy has been fulfilled. The *Roman* armies destroyed Jerusalem and its Temple in 70 A.D. So this ruler will be ruler of the *Roman* empire—or of its modern equivalent, the European Union. (The Roman Empire stretched from England to the eastern Mediterranean, and so does the EU.)

Summary

So the meaning of *Daniel 9:27* appears to be that a powerful EU President will enforce a seven-year treaty between Israel and others. The treaty may be negotiated by the United Nations or the United States or even by the Palestinians and Israelis themselves, but it will be *enforced* by European peacekeeping forces.

The starter-flag for the race to the end of the age

And *that*, the Israel treaty enforced by Europe, is the starter-signal for the final seven years. Read *Daniel 9:27* again: that is what it says.

Armageddon

The seven years ends in Armageddon, though Gabriel does not say so. (Armageddon is not mentioned by name until *Revelation 16:16* nearly at the end of the Bible.)

Our seven-year timescale

So here is our seven-year base-line, shown vertically at a scale of two centimetres to a year, down the right-hand side of the next page. I have added to it the 3½ year mid-point, at which Gabriel says the EU ruler will stop the sacrifices.   The sacrifices can only take place at the Jerusalem Temple, and currently there is no Temple. The one that Jesus knew was destroyed by the Romans in 70 A.D., and the Muslims' Dome

Daniel
(timescale)

Treaty enforced by
peacekeepers sent by
EU leader keeps Jewish
and Palestinian
extremists apart
(start of final
seven years)

1 year

2 years

3 years

3½   erection of
abomination
of desolation

4 years

5 years

6 years

7 years.
Armageddon.

Question:

In Dan. 3:21, why was Daniel not harmed by the flames of the fiery furnace?

Answer on page 9.

Diagram 1 of 12

of the Rock now stands on the Temple site. So there will have to be a new Temple by the time the 3½ year mid-point is reached. Then the "abomination of desolation" will be erected. (What is the "abomination of desolation"? It is an image of the antichrist. More about that later in this book.)

Fulfilment impossible? Not any more!

Here is an astonishing fact:- from 135 A.D. (when the Romans finally drove the Jews out of Israel) until 1948 (when the State of Israel was brought into existence by a majority-vote of the United Nations General Assembly) there was no Israel. And from 476 A.D. (when the last Emperor in Rome was deposed by the Goths) until 1957 (when the European Economic Community—now the European Union or EU—was formed by the Treaty of Rome) there was nothing equivalent to the ancient Roman Empire.

So for nearly 1900 years it was *impossible* for this prophecy of a European leader enforcing a treaty for Israel to be fulfilled. There was no united Europe and no Israel. No wonder theologians said, "It must be taken symbolically, for it cannot be literally fulfilled". But it could be literally fulfilled today, and the concept of foreign peacekeepers is one we know today. The pieces of the jigsaw puzzle are falling into place.

Antiochus Epiphanes

Many Bible scholars allege that all the prophecies in *Dan 9:27* were fulfilled by the end of the reign of the Greek king Antiochus Epiphanes (164 B.C.) or, at the latest, by 70 A.D. when the Romans sacked the Temple and Jerusalem. These views will be looked at in Chapter 11.

In *Dan. 11:31* there is an "abomination of desolation" reference which seems to be destined to be fulfilled *twice:* once by Antiochus Epiphanes and then a second time by the antichrist. It is as if the persecution imposed by Antiochus Epiphanes was a sort of dress-rehearsal or preview of the persecution which will be imposed by the antichrist. Leave these thoughts until Chapter 11: otherwise they can be confusing.

Let's move on

Now let us turn to the words of Jesus found in *Matthew 24* and (in a shorter but very similar form) in *Mark 13*.

- - - - -

Chapter 2

Jesus' Prophecy in *Matthew 24* and *Mark 13*

Jesus leaves the Temple

Jesus had just had a big dispute with the Pharisees in the Jerusalem Temple. He had called them hypocrites and offspring of vipers, and stormed out of the Temple, heading for the Mount of Olives. As he left, he predicted the destruction of the Temple, with "not one stone left upon another" *(Matt. 24:2; Mk. 13:2)* and that is what happened in 70 A.D., because the gold ornamentation of the Temple melted in the fires of destruction, and it is said that the Roman soldiers pulled the masonry apart stone by stone to get at the gold. (The present Wailing Wall is not part of the Temple; it is part of the retaining wall supporting the built-up plateau on which the Temple stood.)

The Olivet discourse

On the Mount of Olives, some of his closest friends asked him, "What will be the sign of your coming?" (Many people expected him to come as conquering hero.) He replied with a long explanation, recorded in *Mk. 13* and in more detail in *Matt. 24*. He spoke of the coming of false Christs, wars, rumours of wars, famines and earthquakes, and likened these to the *beginning* of the labour-pains of childbirth. He told how his followers would experience persecution and martyrdom, and there would be false prophets and increase of wickedness, but the Gospel of the Kingdom of God would be "preached to the whole world" (as is happening today through radio and satellite television) "and then the end will come" *(Matt. 24:5-14; Mk. 13:6-13)*.

I think those who cry, "There are wars in the Middle East, wars and famine in Africa, earthquakes in Asia—the end is nigh!" are jumping the gun a bit. Tell them to go back and be ready for the starter-flag in *Dan. 9:27*, on page 4 of this book.

Abomination and tribulation

But then (in *Matt. 24:15* and *21* and in *Mk. 13:14* and *19*) Jesus gives a very specific warning:-

When you see standing in the holy place [i.e. *the Jerusalem Temple*] the abomination of desolation, spoken of through the prophet Daniel—let the reader understand—then let those in Judea [*the district close to Jerusalem*] flee to the mountains. ... For then there will be great distress (or tribulation) unequalled from the beginning of the world until now—and never to be equalled again. *(Matt. 24:15, 21.)*

The reader who has read Chapter 1 of this book *will* understand what Jesus was referring to. We saw it on page 6.

Timescale
And so we can put a line parallel to our "Daniel" base-line, as we develop our "prophecies in parallel" diagram on page 9.

Rapture!
(The Rapture is the moment when all true Christians are finally snatched up out of this world to be with Jesus.)

Jesus warns again of false prophets, and then states:

Immediately after the tribulation of those days, the sun will be darkened, the moon will not give its light, the stars will fall, and the heavenly bodies will be shaken. *At that time* the sign of the Son of Man [*Jesus himself*] will appear in the sky, and all the nations of the earth will mourn. They will see the Son of Man coming on the clouds of the sky, with power and great glory, and he will send his angels with a loud **trumpet** call, and they will gather his elect from the four winds, from one end of heaven to the other. *(Matt. 24:29-31.)*

There's the Rapture!

(Please read on, even if you feel certain I am wrong. There is more to be said.)

But when?
The problem is, we don't know how far along our line to put the "gathering of the elect". But don't put it at the end: leave room for something else—but Jesus does not tell us what happens next. (Why should he? The Christians are out of it.) I shall argue from the book of *Revelation* that what happens next will be the seven Bowls of Divine Wrath, and then Armageddon (with the "Marriage-Supper of the Lamb" taking place in heaven while the Wrath is poured on earth) but there is nothing of that in Matthew's Gospel. Nor in Mark's Gospel. Jesus simply ended his chronology without going any further.

Matthew, Mark	Daniel *(timescale)*

Treaty enforced by
peacekeepers sent by
EU leader keeps Jewish
and Palestinian
extremists apart
(start of final
seven years)

*Question on page 5: why was Daniel
not harmed by the flames of the fiery
furnace in Dan. 3:21?*

1 year

*Answer: because he was not thrown in.
Shadrach, Meshach and Abednego
were thrown in and were miraculously
saved from harm, but Daniel was not
thrown in. He was later thrown to the
lions and was miraculously saved from
harm on that occasion: Dan. 6:16-22.*

2 years

3 years

abomination of
desolation in
the Temple in
Jerusalem

3½   erection
of abomination
of desolation

G
R
E
A
T

4 years

T
R
I
B
U
L
A
T
I
O
N

5 years

6 years

sun and moon
dark, stars fall,
angels gather
the elect

Diagram 2 of 12

7 years.
Armageddon.

So I can only show this as vaguely along the line—but not at the end of the seven years. As Jesus tells us in *Matt. 24:36* and *Mk. 13:32*, "No-one knows about that day or hour, not even the angels in heaven, not even the Son, but only the Father". But Jesus also told his followers to look out for the signs *(Matt. 24:33* and *Mk. 13:29)* "When you see all these things, you know that it is near, right at the door".

Jesus did not know the date his Father had decreed for the beginning of the final seven years—and at the date this page goes to the printers (end of November, 2006) nor do we. But it is up to us to recognise it when it comes: *1 Thessalonians 5:2-4* "The day of the Lord will come like a thief in the night ... but you are not in darkness so that this day should surprise you like a thief".

Dan. 9:27 gives seven years notice of the termination of this age. It is not seven years notice of the Rapture, but of the termination of the desolation-birthpangs, at the end of which the new age, the millennium, is born.

- - - - -

Watch the news: fill in the date of the European enforcement of the Israel 7-yr treaty when it happens.

Date:- ....

Having filled in that date, add three and a half years, and fill in the date that the erection of the abomination of desolation in the Temple in Jerusalem is to be expected.

Date:- ....

It would not particularly surprise me if President George W. Bush did what his predecessor Bill Clinton narrowly failed to do, and brokered a peace treaty between Israel and the Palestinians before the end of his Presidency in December, 2008. On the other hand, there is no reason at all why these things *must* happen in this generation.

Chapter 3

Jesus' Prophecy according to *Luke*

Split discourse

The discourse which is given as a single account in *Matthew*, and also in *Mark*, is split in two in *Luke*. The part about the moment of the Rapture (as I have interpreted it—knowing that thousands will disagree with me, but please hear me out!) is in a brief form in *Luke 17:20-37;* but the main account is in *Luke 21*.

The account in *Luke 21* begins in the same way as the accounts in *Matthew* and *Mark:* false Christs, wars, revolutions, earthquakes, famines (and plagues) and persecution, and for some, martyrdom *(Luke 21:8-19)*. But then Luke says *(Luke 21:20-21* and *23-24)*:

> When you see Jerusalem surrounded by armies, you will know that its desolation is near. Then let those who are in Judea flee to the mountains. ... There will be great distress in the land and wrath against this people. They will fall by the sword and be taken as prisoners to all the nations. Jerusalem will be trampled on by the gentiles until the times of the gentiles are fulfilled.

What Luke is reporting here is a prophecy by Jesus of the fall of Jerusalem, which was fulfilled in 70 A.D. Or is Luke writing after 70 A.D., and if so is he applying the words of Jesus to the fall of Jerusalem, and saying, "Look: it came true!" I don't know. Note that Luke makes no mention of the "abomination of desolation".

But then in verse 25 Luke comes back into line with what Matthew and Mark have said:

> There will be signs in the sun, moon and stars. ... *And then* they will see the Son of Man coming in a cloud with power and great glory. When these things begin to take place, stand up and lift up your heads, because your redemption is drawing near. *(Luke 21:25-28.)*

And verse 35 adds: "It will come upon all those who live on the face of the whole earth". *This* is not just confined to Jerusalem.

Timescale
So Luke's contribution to our system of parallel lines is only a very short one.

Comment
There is no doubt that Luke's account differs materially from those given by Matthew and Mark.   Whether, when Luke speaks of the fall of Jerusalem, he is recounting a different prophecy which Jesus gave at some other time, or whether Luke is muddling up two conversations, or whether he is deliberately moulding what he remembers, in order to make it fit the Romans' destruction of the city and Temple in 70 A.D., we cannot tell.   Maybe it is a bit of all three.

This does not worry me too much.   Speaking as a lawyer who has occasionally had to cross-examine witnesses in court, I can say that if all the witnesses tell exactly the same story, I suspect that they have got together beforehand and concocted it!   I *expect* independent witnesses to vary in how they remember details.   The evidence in *Luke 21:12-19* is parallel, point by point, with the evidence given in *Matt. 10:17-22*, but Matthew places it much earlier in Jesus' ministry.   Yet a study of the accounts given by Matthew, Mark and Luke will show that in *some* of the details Mark's account is parallel to Luke's, and Matthew's is the odd one out.   (To check this, compare the points A-P across the three columns in Appendix 1 on page 117, where these three accounts are set out in parallel.)

Remember too that Luke may not have been there when Jesus spoke on the Mount of Olives, so he may well have received his information second-hand.

John
The only one of the four gospel-writers who definitely *was* there was John (expressly mentioned in *Mk. 13:3*) but he makes no mention of what Jesus said on this occasion.   John's quotation of Jesus' words, "In my Father's house are many dwellings.   ...   I go to prepare a place for you.   And if I go and prepare a place for you, I will come again and receive you to myself" *(Jn. 14:2-3)* gives no idea of *when* and therefore will not appear on our "timescale" diagram.

- - - - -

Luke	Matthew, Mark	Daniel *(timescale)*

Treaty enforced by
peacekeepers sent by
EU leader keeps Jewish
and Palestinian
extremists apart
(start of final
seven years)

1 year

2 years

3 years

	abomination of desolation in the Temple in Jerusalem	3½ erection of abomination of desolation
	G	4 years
	R	
	E	
	A	
	T	
	T	
	R	
	I	5 years
	B	
	U	
	L	
	A	
	T	
	I	
	O	
	N	6 years
signs in sun, moon and stars	sun and moon dark, stars fall, angels gather the elect	

7 years.
Armageddon.

Diagram 3 of 12

Interpretations and Terminology

Students of prophecy can be divided into preterists, historicists, futurists and idealists. There are also chiliasts and mockers.

Preterists   say prophecy was for the people of Biblical times and is not for us today.

Historicists   claim that the references to 1,260 days in the book of *Revelation* signify 1,260 years which can be traced in world history.

Futurists   take the prophecies more literally and look forward to the return of Jesus at his Second Coming.

Idealists   hold the opinion that prophecies are stories with a moral, about the fight between good and evil: their meaning is "Fight the good fight", "Never give up", and so on.

Chiliasts   believe a golden age will come, but it has nothing to do with religion. Communism was a chiliasm.

Mockers   say it's all rubbish.

This book takes the futurist view.

- - -

The Bible says there will be a millennium, 1,000 years of peace: but futurists argue over this, and they divide into a-millennialists, post-millennialists and pre-millennialists.

A-millennialists   do not believe there will *literally* be 1,000 years of peace. Some of them say it means peace in their hearts through being Christians.

Post-millennialists	believe a golden age will come when nations will live together in peace: and *after* that, Jesus will return.
Pre-millennialists	interpret the prophecies more strictly-literally and say there will be a final seven years containing a time of tribulation leading to Armageddon and the return of Jesus, before the millennium.

This book takes the pre-millennialist view.

- - -

Pre-millennialists split into pre-tribulationists, post-tribulationists, mid-tribulationists and (a recent development) pre-wrathers.

Pre-tribulationists	believe that the Rapture (the prophesied event in which all true Christians are caught up out of this world to be with Jesus) will occur *before the beginning* of the final seven years. Many pre-tribulationists are *dispensationalists*—they say that there is an Old Dispensation (from Moses to Jesus, with sacrifices at the Jerusalem Temple according to the Old Testament Law) and a New Dispensation (from Jesus to the Rapture) and after the Rapture God will return to the Old Dispensation (with sacrifices, which the antichrist will stop) for the final seven years.
Post-tribulationists	argue that the Rapture is at the end of the seven years, so Christians have to go through the tribulation, and then they go up to be with Jesus but they come straight back *with* him for his Second Coming and the millennium.

Mid-tribulationists   believe the Rapture is in the middle of (or sometime during) the final seven years.

Pre-wrathers (who are a sort of mid-tribulationist) believe Christians will have to go through the tribulation (which is to some extent the wrath of Satan) but will not have to go through the Wrath of God which will be inflicted upon all unbelievers.

The four alternatives can be shown diagrammatically, thus, the bottom line representing the final seven years in each case.

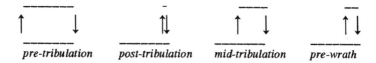

pre-tribulation   post-tribulation   mid-tribulation   pre-wrath

"Pre-tribulation" goes up in the Rapture before the seven years begins; "post-tribulation" goes up at the end and straight down again with our Lord's coming in glory; "mid-tribulation" goes up about halfway through; and "pre-wrath" goes up at some point quite late in the second half of the seven years.

This book takes the pre-wrath view.

- - - - -

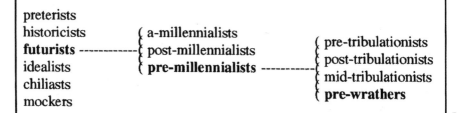

preterists
historicists   (a-millennialists
futurists -----------{ post-millennialists   (pre-tribulationists
idealists   (**pre-millennialists** ----------{ post-tribulationists
chiliasts   { mid-tribulationists
mockers   (**pre-wrathers**

And finally there is *replacement theology* which teaches that God has finished with Israel, so references in prophecy to Israel do not mean Israel, they mean the Church, which has replaced Israel in God's Plan for this planet. I entirely reject this. I believe Israel means Israel.

Chapter 4

Accounts in *Revelation,* etc.

I am afraid this chapter is going to be complicated—as well as controversial. I'll make it as easy and as clear as I can.

The concurrent approach
The book of *Revelation* tells of seven Seals and seven Trumpets. Some people try to argue that they are two accounts of the same series of events, and so they would put them into the order

Seal 1;	1st. Trumpet
Seal 2;	2nd. Trumpet
Seal 3;	3rd. Trumpet
Seal 4;	4th. Trumpet
Seal 5;	5th. Trumpet
Seal 6;	6th. Trumpet
Seal 7;	7th. Trumpet.

This is the "concurrent" approach.

The consecutive approach
Others would allege that the seven Trumpets come *after* the seven Seals. (This is the order they appear in the text of *Revelation*). Thus:-

Seals 1, 2, 3, 4, 5, 6 and 7, *(Rev. 6:2 - 8:1)*
and then Trumpets 1, 2, 3, 4, 5, 6 and 7. *(Rev. 8:7 - 11:15)*
This is the "consecutive" approach.

The newspaper approach
I reject both these theories and go for the "newspaper" approach. It's like this. Suppose on page 8 of a newspaper there is a report of operations of American ground forces in Iraq, and on page 9 of the same newspaper there is an account of the operations of American helicopters in Iraq. They are two separate items. It does not follow that what is reported on page 9 happened *after* what is on page 8. Either of them may be first, or they may be two aspects of one operation, or two operations which overlapped, or two at the same time but in different places—we cannot tell, unless the reports themselves tell us. In *Revelation*, treat the "seven Seals" report and the "seven Trumpets" report

as two *overlapping* reports. (But keep the Seals in order, and keep the Trumpets in order. For instance, the second Seal can come before the first Trumpet, but the second Seal certainly cannot come before the first Seal.) After scratching my head quite a lot over the Seals and Trumpets, I have concluded that the most likely order of events is as follows:-

Rev. 6:2	Seal 1	(white horse: conqueror)
6:4	Seal 2	(red horse: war)
8:7	Trumpet 1	(one third of trees and all grass burnt)
6:6	Seal 3	(black horse: famine)
8:9	Trumpet 2	(one third of ships and fish destroyed)
8:11	Trumpet 3	(one third of fresh waters polluted)
6:8	Seal 4	(pale horse: plague and death)
8:12	Trumpet 4	(one third of day and night gone—i.e. shortened)
9:1	Trumpet 5	(Satan falls from heaven onto earth)
6:10	Seal 5	(cries in heaven: "How long?")
		[Erection of the "abomination of desolation" comes here.]
9:13	Trumpet 6	(two hundred million soldiers from the east, at the River Euphrates)
6:12	Seal 6	(great earthquake, sun dark, stars fall)
11:15	Trumpet 7	(earthquake the same as Seal 6; lightning, great hailstorm—and Rapture at the last Trumpet)
8:1	Seal 7	(silence—
16:1		and then **seven Bowls** of Divine Wrath).

I had better give some explanations and reasons for all that!

Prophecies of destruction in *Revelation* and elsewhere

Immense destruction is foretold in the book of *Revelation*, with the sun dark and the stars falling (and remember that we saw on page 8 that Jesus also said that these things would happen). And we could add the Old Testament prophets Isaiah "The Lord is going to lay waste the Earth and devastate it." *(Is. 24:1)* and Jeremiah "I looked at the Earth, and it was formless and empty; and at the heavens, and their light was gone. I looked at the mountains, and they were quaking." *(Jer. 4:23-24)*. And Habakkuk "He stood, and shook the Earth. ... The ancient mountains crumbled." *(Hab. 3:6)*. And Haggai "I will once more shake the heavens and the Earth." *(Hag. 2:6)* and Psalm 18 "The Earth trembled and quaked, and the foundations of the mountains shook." *(Ps. 18:7)*.

Such things just don't happen in the normal course of events! They have never been known in human history. Or have they? Homer, writing probably around 1000 B.C. about the Trojan Wars which were probably in about 1200 B.C., said, "The gods clashed with a mighty din, and round about great heaven *pealed as with a trumpet*". (ἀμφὶ δὲ σάλπιγξεν μέγας οὐρανός) Homer, *The Iliad*, xxi, 388. Did he know of something that we today do not know of?

Could such things ever happen?   There seems to be a missing ingredient.   And the missing ingredient which could cause such devastation is an asteroid or bolide or a comet. (Remember those three as A-B-C.)

Asteroids (and bolides and comets)

It never ceases to surprise me that many Bible students who study the book of *Revelation* never seem to read a book on this aspect of astronomy, and many astronomers seem scarcely aware of the book of *Revelation*. Let us bang their heads together and see what comes out.

Asteroids

Asteroids are lumps of rock which go round the sun like the Earth does. There are thousands of them.   Whether they are the remains of a shattered planet or whether they are bits which never came together to form a planet, is not known.

Comets

Comets come from far out in the solar system.   They swing round close to the sun and then fly out again.

Bolide

Bolide is a more general word meaning meteorites and any other sort of space-rock falling onto this planet—so it includes asteroids and comets.

When these things hit Earth's atmosphere, they burn up as "shooting stars" if they are tiny, but larger ones explode like nuclear bombs because of the sheer friction and heat generated when they encounter Earth's atmosphere at a speed of maybe 50,000 miles (80,000 kilometres) per hour.   One which exploded over Tunguska (in Siberia) in 1908 devastated a patch of forest 25 miles (40 kilometres) across.

The Jupiter crash

In 1994, a comet crashed into Jupiter.   Jupiter is a much larger planet than Earth.   At certain times of the year it can be seen like a bright star (though not as bright as the Morning-and-Evening Star, which is Venus) and with strong binoculars it is possible to see four little moons circling round Jupiter.

In 1992 the comet known as Comet Shoemaker-Levy 9 (named after the astronomers who discovered it, and numbered 9 because it was the ninth one that this team of astronomers had discovered) was seen close to Jupiter. It had become caught in Jupiter's gravity. Astronomers watched through their telescopes as it circled round Jupiter for a further two years, and they saw it break into twenty-one pieces. Then, over the period of seven days from 16th to 22nd July, 1994, those twenty-one pieces all crashed into Jupiter. Most of those impacts made such explosions that they were seen (and photographed) through telescopes on planet Earth. Scientists say that if a space-rock as big as that comet were to hit the Earth, it would destroy the Earth.

Could there be an Earth-crash?
Astronomers have become worried that it could happen to our planet. (Some of them say it has happened before and that this is what brought about the extinction of the dinosaurs.) They have set up an organisation to track asteroids, but they admit they have no way of stopping a big one that comes our way.

Asteroids large and small
Asteroids vary in size. The smallest ones are smaller than a football (and harmless to us) while the largest one, called Ceres, is more than four hundred miles across. Several hundred with a diameter of more than half a mile are known, and when one of these comes near Earth, the press usually gives a dramatic headline, only to forget it a few days later. For example:-

End of the world is odds on   *Sunday Express, 23 June, 1991*
Doomsday team watch for asteroid Armageddon *Daily Mail, 1 Jan. 2000*
The day the Earth nearly caught fire   *Daily Mail, 21 June, 2002*
The end is nigh   *Daily Mail, 25 July, 2002*
Earth could be on course for asteroid collision *The Times, 3 Sept. 2003*
Target Earth!   *Daily Mail, 3 Sept. 2003*

Revelation: the first two Seals.
Now let us return to *Revelation*, and to the list of events which we saw on page 18.

	Revelation	Matthew, Mark	Daniel *(timescale)*

1st seal: white horse: emergence of a great leader

Treaty enforced by peacekeepers sent by EU leader keeps Jewish and Palestinian extremists apart (start of final seven years)

1 year

2nd seal: red horse signifying war

2 years

3 years

Matt., Mk.

abomination of desolation in the Temple in Jerusalem

3½ erection of abomination of desolation

G
R
E
A
T

4 years

T
R
I
B
U
L
A
T
I
O
N

5 years

Luke

6 years

signs in sun, moon and stars

sun and moon dark, stars fall, angels gather the elect

7 years. Armageddon

Diagram 4 of 12

The first Seal (a statesmanlike leader, and Peace)

Unsealing the first Seal *(Rev. 6:2)* reveals a conqueror on a white horse. Let us assume that this is the great EU leader that we saw on page 4 enforcing peace for Israel. (If he is not that leader, the whole of my argument will fall apart, so *please* assume here that he is! Treat this like a jig-saw puzzle: if this piece is placed here, a picture will come together—and otherwise it won't.) So he brings Peace, which is intended to be for seven years—we saw on page 3 that this is a seven-year treaty—and so at last Israel (and also the Palestinians) can relax.

The fields in Israel are planted. The crops are growing. There is expectation of a good harvest. But...

The second Seal (look to the North: it's War!)

But the Peace doesn't last, because the unsealing of the second Seal *(Rev. 6:4)* reveals the red horse of War.

Here is a detail to keep in mind: the prophet Joel foresees *four* waves of invaders like four plagues of locusts *(Joel 1:4)*.

An Attack on Israel from the North (Ezekiel's and Joel's Accounts)

The prophet Ezekiel describes a sudden unexpected invasion of Israel from the North *(Ezek. 38 and 39)* led by "Gog from the land of Magog" *(Ezek. 38:2 et seq.)*. Some people say "Gog" means Russia.

But why do I suggest that this attack is at *this* time, corresponding to the opening of the second Seal? I say it because Ezekiel says the invaders come against a people living in safety *(Ezek. 38:8)* ... rich in livestock and goods *(Ezek. 38:12)*. So this must be the *first* of Joel's four waves, for it does not come over already-devastated land. It seems to be the same event as that described in *Joel 2:3* "Before them the land is like the Garden of Eden, behind them, a desert waste. Nothing escapes them." In *Ezek. 38:9* we are told that the invaders will be like a cloud covering the land.

Israel holds a National Day of Prayer: *Joel 2:15.*

And then something awful happens to the invading army.

Fire falls from the heavens

Ezek. 38:22-23 tells us it is by the hand of God: "I shall rain on him, and on his troops, and on the many nations with him, a torrential rain,

Revelation	Matthew, Mark	Daniel *(timescale)*
1st seal: white horse: emergence of a great leader		Treaty enforced by peacekeepers sent by EU leader keeps Jewish and Palestinian extremists apart (start of final seven years)
		1 year

Joel | **Ezekiel**

| Joel's 1st
wave of
"locusts" | Israel is invaded
by "Gog" from
the north: but the
invading army is
destroyed in a
single day by fire
from heaven. 7
months is needed
to bury the dead.
And they stink. | 2nd seal: red horse
signifying war | 2 years |
| | | | 3 years |

Note:- In the next version of this chart,
Ezekiel will be moved across into the
Matthew-and-Mark column, to make
room for further columns on the left.

Matt., Mk.

	abomination of desolation in the Temple in Jerusalem	3½ erection of abomination of desolation
	G	4 years
	R	
	E	
	A	
	T	
	T	
	R	
	I	5 years
	B	
	U	
	L	
	A	
	T	
	I	
	O	
	N	6 years

Diagram 5 of 12

Luke

| signs in
sun, moon
and stars | sun and moon
dark, stars fall,
angels gather
the elect | |

| | | 7 years.
Armageddon |

with hailstones, fire and brimstone" *(Ezek. 38:22)*. (In some modern translations of the Bible, "fire and brimstone" is translated as "burning sulphur". It is a substance which often comes out of volcanoes when they erupt.) ... "And they will know that I am the Lord" *(Ezek. 38:23)*. Those last nine words show that this comes from God and not from nuclear warfare.

Hailstones and fire do not normally go together. "Hailstones" here may mean "hail of stones"—bolides. The Hebrew phrase in *Ezek. 38:22* is וְגָפְרִית אֵשׁ אֶלְגָּבִישׁ וְאַבְנֵי *(v'abney elgabeesh eysh v'gaphreeth)*. It means: "&-stones-of crystal *[that could be ice or rock]* fire &-sulphur".

And where would such a devastating shower suddenly come from? It could be debris sucked in by Earth's gravity from a passing comet or asteroid which gives planet Earth a near-miss, with Earth's gravity sucking thousands of fragments off the asteroid, and they come to Earth as meteorites (or, more likely, go white-hot and then explode in the atmosphere above the Earth). So here we have a scientific basis for what would otherwise seem to be a pretty far-fetched prophecy.

It has happened before: it appears to have happened to Sodom and Gomorrah *(Gen. 19:24)* and it may be what killed 185,000 soldiers in Sennacherib's army in a single night in 701 B.C. *(2 Kings 19:35)*. There is a somewhat questionable theory that there was an asteroid-strike at that time on some uninhabited part of our planet which knocked Earth from an orbit of 360 days into its present orbit of 365¼ days.

And Almighty God chooses the time and place for it to fall—right onto the middle of the invading army. Little or nothing of the army is left. *Joel 2:20* says, "I will drive the northern army far from you ... with its front columns going into the Dead Sea (or eastern sea) and those in the rear into the Mediterranean (or western sea). And its stench will go up; its smell will rise." *Ezek. 39:12* says it will take seven months just to bury the dead. Here *(Ezek. 38:22)* and in the Sodom and Gomorrah account *(Gen. 19:22-24)* and in the account of Sennacherib's disaster *(2 Kings 19:35)* we see that God has all these things under his control.

NASA

In January of 2005, the North American Space Agency (NASA) launched a space-probe towards the comet Tempel 1 which passed us eighty-three million miles away. On July 4th., 2005, they hit it, as they

| Asteroid Theory | Revelation | Daniel *(timescale)* |

1st seal: white horse: emergence of a great leader

Treaty enforced by peacekeepers sent by EU leader keeps Jewish and Palestinian extremists apart (start of final seven years)

1 year

Joel   ## Ezekiel

Joel's 1st wave of "locusts" | asteroid's near-miss showers meteorites onto the invaders *(Jews see this as a miracle and immediately rebuild the Temple)* | **2nd seal: red horse** signifying war | Israel is invaded by "Gog" from the north: but the invading army is destroyed in a single day by fire from heaven. 7 months is needed to bury the dead. And they stink. | 2 years

---
To unbelievers:- **THE CHALLENGE OF GOG.** Believe what you read in this book when you see Israel's northern invaders destroyed by *fire from heaven.*
---

3 years

Matt., Mk.

abomination of desolation in the Temple in Jerusalem | 3½ erection of abomination of desolation

G
R
E
A
T

4 years

T
R
I
B
U
L
A
T
I
O
N

5 years

6 years

Luke

signs in sun, moon and stars | sun and moon dark, stars fall, angels gather the elect

Diagram 6 of 12

7 years. Armageddon

had planned. They were accurate to within fifty yards (forty-six metres). (This was part of their research into how to divert one of these things if it comes uncomfortably close.) But do you think Almighty God is less capable of such accuracy than NASA?

The effect in Jerusalem

What is likely to be the effect in Jerusalem, of the destruction of their enemies' army? It seems to me the Jews are likely to say, "It's a miracle! Our prayer has been answered! Our God is with us!" (Or in the words of *Ezek. 39:22*, "From that day forward the house of Israel will know that I am the Lord their God".)

And so we can imagine these super-inspired Jews seizing the Temple Mount from the Arabs, removing the Muslims' Dome of the Rock (which stands on the Temple site) and beginning the rebuilding of their Temple to their God who has just rescued them. ... Remember please that this paragraph is only my speculation, but it seems to follow logically enough from what Joel and Ezekiel have said.

The effect in the invaders' nations

If a country's entire army is wiped out, the public unrest in that country is likely to be such that its government will not survive for long. The countries from which the invading troops came may well be left without any effective form of government, except in areas where Islam takes control.

The menace still lurking in space

Remember that asteroid (or that comet—whichever it is). It's not going to go clean away. It's caught in Earth's gravity and can't get free. It goes away like a ball on a piece of elastic, but it will be drawn back.

- - - - -

Chapter 5

Revelation, continued

It's back! The asteroid has returned, and this time it's closer, as Earth's gravity draws it in. This time, we can all *hear* it, like a trumpet. (Remember what Homer said on page 19 above? Now we can know that experience for ourselves. This is the first of the seven Trumpets.)

The first Trumpet
Debris flies off the asteroid: another immense shower of white-hot meteorites impacts across the Earth. This is no localised bombardment of a few square kilometres in the Middle East! *Rev. 8:7* tells us, "There came hail and fire, mixed with blood ... one third of the Earth was burned up, one third of the trees were burned up, and all the green grass was burned up". ("Hail" being "hail of fiery stones" again.)

So a swathe of destruction is cut across one third of the Earth. Many trees and "all the green grass" are burnt. And where are the world's great grasslands? The prairies and the Russian steppes. They include the world's premier wheat-producing lands.

The third Seal (famine)
If all that green (not yet golden for harvest) landscape becomes blackened stubble, it is hardly surprising that the unsealing of the third Seal *(Rev. 6:6)* reveals a merchant giving a cry which we can paraphrase into modern terms as, "A loaf of bread for a day's wages". But he adds, "Don't damage the oil and the wine"—and maybe that indicates the latitude for this disaster. The grasslands are devastated, but the olive groves and vineyards further south escape.

Destruction on this scale would be such a blow to the American economy that the United States would cease to be a World Power. (This may be why America scarcely appears at all in these "End Times" prophecies.) The President and the Federal Government would not necessarily survive.

Line of flight
Could England be in the line of fire? I guess it might. The swathe of destruction would be likely to cross the planet from east to west (or from

west to east) with a deviation of up to twenty-three and a half degrees to the north or to the south depending on the time of year, the time of day and various other factors.

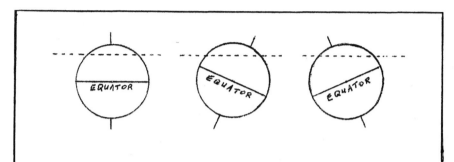

Possible trajectories of incoming bolides. Remember that the solar system is shaped rather like a plate, so these things would come from the general direction of the sun, moon and planets (the zodiac). They would be very unlikely to come from the direction of (for example) the Pole Star, which is in a completely different part of the heavens.

The second Trumpet
Then comes the second Trumpet. This time it is not a widespread shower of debris that falls: it is one solid lump. "Something like a huge mountain, all ablaze, was thrown into the sea" *(Rev. 8:8)*. The shock-wave kills one third of the fish, and there are massive shipping casualties. And if it has crashed into the Atlantic, it will probably have caused a *tsunami*, a tidal wave, sufficient to overwhelm London's Thames barrier and the dykes of Holland, and on the other side of the ocean the lower parts of New York, and such a bang on the Earth's surface will be likely to generate earthquakes affecting earthquake-prone cities such as Tokyo on the opposite side of the globe.

The third Trumpet
"A great star ... blazing like a torch" *(Rev. 8:10)* falls and pollutes the rivers and water supplies. The name of this star *(Rev. 8:11)* is Wormwood (or in the original Greek Αψινθος *Apsinthos*) which means bitterness. A lot of people die because of the bitter water.

Compare this with Science
When the comet Shoemaker-Levy 9 crashed into Jupiter, its twenty-one fragments crashed over a period of seven days. Following this pattern,

we can expect that the bolides of the first three Trumpets (if they are bolides from a comet or an asteroid) will come in similarly-quick succession. So the greater part of the leading nations of the world will have been suddenly transformed—or devastated—in just a few days.

The fourth Seal (Death)

Unsealing the fourth Seal *(Rev. 6:8)* reveals Death, with power over a quarter of the planet to kill by sword, famine, plague and "the wild beasts".

Yet none of these disasters will completely fulfil the predictions of Isaiah and Jeremiah *(etc.)* which we saw on page 18 above. The big one is yet to come.

The fourth Trumpet

Regarding the fourth Trumpet, we are told *(Rev. 8:12)* "One third of the day was without light, and also one third of the night". Does this mean that there is such pollution that the sun, moon and stars are dimmed by one third? It may do: *Joel 2:10* and *3:15* (but not *Joel 2:31* which is a different event) mention a dimming of the stars.

Or does it mean that the Earth has received such a bang that it spins faster, going from one midnight to the next in sixteen hours instead of twenty-four? (There are problems with this theory. It would result in the "1,260 days" which we shall see later in the book of *Revelation*—see pages 37 and 52 below—being completed in about two and one third years instead of three and a half years.)

At present, no-one knows what this prophecy means. When it happens, we shall be able to say, "So *that's* what it meant!" But at present it is outside human experience.

Woe: the fifth Trumpet

The account of the fifth Trumpet, too, tells of something outside human experience. *Rev. 9:1* tells us of a falling star *which opens the bottomless pit*, and "locusts with stings like scorpions" come out, following a leader called Abaddon (or Apollyon) which means "destroyer". *(Rev. 9:1-11.)* They torment people for five months: and this is known as "**the first woe**". *(Rev. 9:12.)*

Who (not just *what* but also *who*) is this falling star? This star (another piece of the asteroid, although the main body of the asteroid does not fall—yet) is different. It is a lump of space-rock—but it is not *merely* a lump of space-rock. Here we seem to see the fulfilment of Isaiah's prophecy *(Is. 14:12)* "How you have fallen from heaven, O morning star (or Lucifer: the Authorised Version says Lucifer, though most other translations do not mention a name) son of the dawn! You have been cast down to the Earth".

Here is Satan, the chieftain of what Saint Paul calls the "spiritual forces of evil in the heavenly realms" *(Eph. 6:12)* and he is thrown down to Earth. At this moment he will still be a spirit, without a flesh-and-blood body: but he will need one. We are about to see the Incarnation of Satan.

We are familiar with the Incarnation of Jesus. He came as a baby in Bethlehem and was brought up by his mother Mary and her husband Joseph who was a carpenter. But an incarnation like that would not satisfy Satan. He would prefer to have the world's top job.

Overview of the World

Before we continue, let us back-track, just for two pages, to the beginning of the final seven years, the beginning of the final "week" prophesied by Gabriel in *Dan. 9:27* which we saw on page 2. Let us add more detail, to get a clearer picture—bearing in mind that although the *outline* is given in Scripture, the *details*, and the *application* of the facts to the world of the twenty-first century, are only my speculation.

I do not have the gift of prophecy, either of the Scriptures or of the movements of asteroids. But after reading the Bible and factual reports of the impact of the comet Shoemaker-Levy 9 onto Jupiter, and after considering the opinions of theologians and astronomers more knowledgeable in their respective fields than myself, I think I'm on the right track.

What we have envisaged is a world of increasing prosperity, with a powerful European leader enforcing peace between Israel and her opponents in the Middle East. It is a world of increasing affluence, leisure, travel, tourism and human rights in the developed Western world, though Islamic fundamentalist terrorism remains a threat: and when an invader attacks Israel from the north, this rich life of pleasure in the west is little affected—indeed, people who do not watch TV News or read serious newspapers will be scarcely aware of it. But then the invader is destroyed by fire from heaven in the form of exploding meteors and crashing meteorites which are more devastating than nuclear bombs.

	Asteroid Theory	Revelation		Daniel *(timescale)*

1st seal: white horse: emergence of a great leader

Treaty enforced by peacekeepers sent by EU leader keeps Jewish and Palestinian extremists apart (start of final seven years)

1 year

Joel
Ezekiel

Joel's 1st swarm of "locusts"	asteroid's near-miss showers meteorites onto the invaders *(Jews see this as a miracle and immediately rebuild the Temple)*	2nd seal: red horse signifying war	Israel is invaded by "Gog" from the north: but the invading army is destroyed in a single day by fire from heaven. 7 months is needed to bury the dead. And they stink.	2 years

asteroid now showers more meteorites & larger bolides

1st trumpet, 3rd seal, 2nd & 3rd trumpets, 4th seal, 4th & 5th trumpets

3 years

Matt., Mk.

abomination of desolation in the Temple in Jerusalem

3½ erection of abomination of desolation

G
R
E
A
T

4 years

T
R
I
B
U
L
A
T
I
O
N

5 years

Luke

signs in sun, moon and stars

sun and moon dark, stars fall, angels gather the elect

6 years

7 years. Armageddon

Diagram 7 of 12

That will be fantastic news-footage if any TV camera-crews survive to show it. Headlines. Scientists will report that a space-rock has passed close by and is now moving away. City-centre open-air preachers who proclaim that it is the judgment of God may draw crowds of a few dozen for a few minutes. ("Repent! Give up your selfish, immoral, dishonest, alcoholic, foul-mouthed, drug-snorting ways and throw yourselves onto the mercy of Jesus who died for repentant sinners"—and the crowd thins out even more.) Scientists will declare that what has happened is a natural phenomenon—a tragedy indeed, but no more so than the destruction of Pompeii by the volcanic eruption of Vesuvius in 79 A.D.

A month later it will all be stale news—boring. There is a big sports event to look forward to.

But then...

But then the asteroid comes back, and *within a single week* the world's grasslands are burnt and their towns devastated (by the first trumpeting shower of bolides) so there will be no wheat for making next year's bread—and the lowland cities of northern America and northern Europe are flooded, millions of fish in the Atlantic's already-depleted fish shoals are floating dead, and millions of tons of shipping has been sunk (by the shock-wave from the second trumpeting bolide)—and across northern Europe people are dying through lack of drinkable water (because of the acid rain caused by the third trumpeting bolide, for these things generate nitric and sulphuric acid, as the scientists know)— and the weather, the climate and even the clocks are awry (after the fourth trumpeting bolide) and there is such lawlessness that people ask whether this is panic-reaction or whether there are devils walking the lands. *All in a single week.*

The Mediterranean region seems to have escaped comparatively lightly. *Rev. 6:6* says, "A litre of wheat for a day's wages, and three litres of barley for a day's wages, and *do not damage the oil and the wine!*" so the olive-and-vineyard latitudes seem to have fared better than the grassland latitudes.

America and Europe and Russia are in political and economic chaos. Africa was impotent with plagues, famines and wars even before these disasters. China seems to have had a lucky escape. The world leaders are at their wits' end as to what to do in this unprecedented disaster. But it is the leader of the European Union who takes control of the situation.

Europe has a good leader—a statesman who has done great and good things—but how is he to cope with *this?*

He looks at the smoking ruin of America. He looks at Russia and her allies: they are without an army and mostly without government. International trade is more or less at a standstill. Then he looks at his own domain, where people are starving through lack of bread, and people are dying from water-pollution. There are calls for his resignation (as there always are in such situations). He is at his wits' end: *what* can he do?

The EU President gets a visitor

At this point the good EU leader is approached by a being who claims to have come down from heaven. (The claim is true: he *has* just been thrown out of heaven: *Rev. 12:9.*) Never has an angel more beautiful been seen, than this glorious shining spirit. And he makes to the good leader the same offer that he made to the humble carpenter nearly two thousand years ago: "You see all these nations? I'll give you *the whole lot* if you'll bow down and worship me." *(Matt. 4:8-9; Luke 4:5-7.)*

The leader *could* refuse the offer, as Jesus did. He *could* pray to God (whom he has never seen) for help, and trust Him to answer. Or he could accept the so-tempting offer of this visitor whom he sees standing before him, offering immediate real help. Here is a firm offer. Surely a bird in the hand is worth two in the bush. "You have come to us from heaven. I bow to you and to your superior wisdom. I accept your offer."

And so the good EU leader becomes a pawn of Satan. He is still a fine politician and a great statesman, and probably a very charming fellow: but now he is *possessed* by Satan himself. He is the antichrist; he is Satan Incarnate—he is Satan (also referred to as "the dragon") in a human body. Muslims call him the Dajjal. If you like, we can call him Son of Satan, in the same way that we refer to Jesus as Son of God—and don't be put off by anyone telling you, "It is not in Satan's nature to have a son".

The fifth Seal (a howling in heaven)

And the unsealing of the fifth Seal reveals a howl going up in heaven from martyrs crying, "How long?" and they are told to wait a little longer "until the number of *[those]* who were to be killed as they had been, was completed" *(Rev. 6:11).*

The mark

"I promised you the world. Go and get it. The way to get world control is to get *economic* control. Look at Russia: ruined economy. Look at America: you've just seen the day the dollar died. Look at Europe. How much wheat can you buy today for a hundred euros? Scarcely any. Look at the world's stock markets—ruined. Even if earthquake-smitten Japan can still make motors, it can find no-one to buy them.

So set up a completely new World Economy, based on the internet—no coins, no notes, no cheques, no plastic cards that can be stolen—everyone's bank number will be printed on their right hand. The credit-debit machines that you will instal everywhere—from the biggest banks and mega-stores to the smallest tea-machines and telephone booths and even the public toilets—will read the palm-print. Set up a system in which every person left alive receives an implanted credit-number on their hand in return for swearing allegiance to me, giving *worship* to me as their supreme leader.

Worship me!

Oh yes! That is one thing I *insist* on. I will not be taken for granted: I require *everyone* to show their gratitude, in a public act of worship, for what I am doing for them. I have come from heaven and I *will* be worshipped, as God. It is something I have long yearned for, and now I come as the God of this world. And I will not be worshipped as a vague disembodied spirit, as so many previous deities have been—because you, my good leader, have bowed the knee to me: you have opened yourself to me: and I shall enter into your innermost being: I *possess* you: henceforth we are one: you are me and I am *you*.

Get me a Temple!

My worship requires a Temple. Not a second-hand one, so I don't particularly want St. Peter's in Rome, nor the Ka'aba in Mecca. I want that brand new one in Jerusalem—but those Jews are just about to begin making sacrifices there to Yahweh (or call him Jehovah if you like) but it's him that I blame for all this trouble. Stop them!

I blame Yahweh and the Jews for all this. Without the Jews, there would have been no middle-east crisis and none of this would ever have happened." (He omits to mention that if the Jews had been left alone in their own land and had not been attacked, none of this would ever have happened.)

Put my image in the Temple!

And so the good leader, now possessed so that he has become Satan Incarnate (though in appearance he has not changed, except that his face may begin to develop a sterner expression) stops the sacrifices and causes an image of himself to be set up in the new Temple. Whether this image will be a statue, a hologram, a clone of himself, or some other type of image, is not yet clear. What *is* clear is that this image is the "abomination of desolation". We saw it in *Dan. 9:27* on page 6, and here is more detail from *Dan. 11:31*, "His armed forces will rise up to desecrate the Temple fortress and will abolish the daily sacrifice. Then they will set up the abomination of desolation." This blasphemous image is an abomination desolating the newly-completed Temple. (We noted *Dan. 11:31* on page 6 as a "double-fulfilment" prophecy. It was fulfilled by Antiochus Epiphanes in the second century B.C. when he sacrificed a pig and built an altar to Jupiter on top of the Temple altar, and it is destined to be fulfilled again by the antichrist when his blasphemous image is erected.)

And *Dan. 9:27* (pages 2-4) tells us when this is. It is at the half-way point of our seven-year period. As we have seen, *Dan. 9:27* gives us two important markers: the peace treaty enforced for Israel marks the beginning of the final seven years; and the stopping of the sacrifices and the erection of the abomination of desolation marks the middle of the seven years.

"Don't put it in the holy of holies where no-one can see it! Tell the fools to put it up high—up there on the pinnacle—so that you ... we ... I can look down on them all, and they will all look up to **me**, whom they will worship! I shall no longer speak of *you*, or of *us*, but only of **me**, for I have possessed you: you are my body."

Beast

Thus did the good leader become the beast.

History repeated

"Here are the instructions for worshipping me. It is the same ceremonial that the Roman emperors used. On an appointed day, which I may call 'the Islam day' [he deliberately uses the Muslim word for "submission"] each year, every person will bow in submission to me and will burn a pinch of incense and will declare that the Emperor (as I shall call myself) is their Lord. This will unite the human race under me as their one Lord and will wipe out conflict—just as the Roman emperors did, only more so. Then they shall place their right hand upon the electronic implanter which gives them their mark—their internet financial access code, their 'www' equivalent or whatever the programmers call it. Those who won't worship me won't get a mark. Let them die."

Second beast (a false prophet)

There is also a second beast—some people say he is a Bishop, or alternatively a Jew—who sees to the erection of the image in the Temple on behalf of the first beast. "He was given power to give breath to the image of the first beast" *[What does that mean? Is it a clone?]* "so that it could speak, and cause all those who refuse to worship the image to be killed" *(Rev. 13:15)*. Take your choice: worship the devil or die.

These leaders will have no hesitation in persecuting these "enemies of the human race", these traitorous Christians standing in the way of World Unity. One of their methods is the same as that which was used by the ancient Roman emperors nineteen hundred years ago to cement the unity of the ancient Roman Empire: everyone will perform sacrifice to The Emperor. Members of the early Christian community who were unwilling to worship the emperor soon divided into four categories: (i) those who submitted and sacrificed, (ii) those who refused and were martyred, (iii) those who refused but escaped martyrdom because either they fled into the desert or they were still *waiting* to be martyred when the current bout of persecution ended, and (iv) those who refused, but, by bribery or other means, obtained a counterfeit certificate saying they had sacrificed. History may well repeat itself.

- - - - -

Phaeton

The Roman poet Ovid, writing *Metamorphoses* in 8 A.D., told the story of Phaeton, who was allowed to drive the sun's chariot for just one day, but he lost control of it and crashed it. *At Phaethon rutilos flamma populante capillos volvitur in praeceps longoque per aera tractu fertur,* "But Phaeton, with flames searing his glowing locks ... went hurtling down through the air, leaving a long trail behind". *(Metamorphoses 2:320.)*

Is this an account of an ancient legend that Ovid had heard, handed down from long-dead ancestors who had *seen* such an event—i.e. the fall of a large flaming meteorite? History does not tell us.

Chapter 6

Great Tribulation

Jewish Reaction
The Jews, horrified at this desecration of their Temple, will not worship him. But he's not going to stand for that.

Persecution begins
"When you see the abomination of desolation standing where it ought not ... let those who are in Judea flee to the mountains..." *(Matt. 24:15-16; Mk. 13:14).* Jesus warned: "Don't even go back to get your coat!" *(Matt. 24:18, paraphrased).* There seems to be a suggestion here of a sudden massacre, with the Jews literally running for their lives.

Treat the book of *Revelation* like a newspaper. Different articles and news-items are on different pages. *Rev. 12* tells us what happens next. Satan—the controlling spirit in the person of the EU leader—makes a determined attempt to persecute the Jews. (This is *Rev. 12:13.* The "woman" in that verse signifies the nation that gave birth to Jesus, i.e. the Jewish nation.) Possibly this attack is the second of Joel's four swarms of locusts *(Joel 1:4).* See how the leader's policy has been changed under Satan's influence: previously he had been trying to protect the Jews, although his enforcement of their seven-year peace treaty had taken a hard knock.

But the Jews flee *(Rev. 12:14)* and are protected in the desert, mysteriously beyond Satan's reach, for "a time, times and half a time", which probably signifies three and a half years, though we do not yet know for certain. *Rev. 12:6* describes this period as 1,260 days.

And then *(Rev. 12:17)* he persecutes the Christians. (Satan hates the Jews because they are part of God's divine plan and they produced Jesus; and Satan hates the Christians because, through Jesus, they have escaped his clutches in eternity.) The beast was given a mouth "to utter proud words and blasphemies and to exercise his authority for a period of forty-two months *[which is three and a half years].* (Rev. 13:5.)* He opened his mouth to blaspheme God *(Rev. 13:6).* He was given power to make war against the saints *[i.e. the real Christians—in contrast to purely nominal Christians, who will support him]* **and to conquer them.**

And he was given authority over every tribe, people, language and nation" *(Rev. 13:7)*.

So, if Satan promised the EU leader the whole world, he has kept his promise—but we shall see shortly what the Asian forces will do.

Christian Reaction

Those Christians who know their Bible will be aware of *Rev. 14:9-11,*

> If any one worships the beast and his image, and receives a mark on their forehead or upon their hand, that person will also drink of the wine of the wrath of God, which is mixed in full strength in the cup of his anger; and will be tormented with fire and brimstone in the presence of the holy angels and in the presence of the Lamb: and the smoke of their torment goes up for ever and ever; and they have no rest day and night, those who worship the beast and his image, and whoever receives the mark of his name.

So they will not worship the antichrist, and so cannot receive his mark. So they cannot buy or sell *(Rev. 13:17)*. Have you taken heed of Joseph's advice to Pharaoh in *Gen. 41:29-36*, to store up, in the good years, food for the bad years? But even if you have, remember that at the time of the siege of Jerusalem in 70 A.D., any closed-up house was seen as a sign that a family might be sheltering in there *with food*. "Break the door down and kill them." But will you still have a house to live in? Or will you have been evicted for non-payment of rent or taxes, because you have no mark and therefore cannot make any payments, no matter how affluent you formerly were? (Or perhaps your home and your store of food got destroyed in the *tsunami*.) Christianity at that time will not be a matter of clapping hands and singing "I'm h-a-p-p-y".

Every true Christian—but most especially those who believed they would be taken up in the Rapture before all this, and so they were not psychologically prepared for it—will be severely shaken. Jesus warned, "Many will fall away" *(Matt. 24:10)*.

The Christians, who have been declared enemies of humanity, worthy of death, cannot even buy bread—not that there is much of that commodity available for *anyone* to buy.

But is there also at this time nuclear war? I don't know yet, but I am inclined to wonder whether the position is that the cosmic onslaughts are in God's hands *(Rev. 16:9* "They blasphemed the name of God who *has the power* over these plagues")* but concurrently there is nuclear war

	Asteroid Theory	Revelation		Daniel *(timescale)*

1st seal: white horse: emergence of a great leader

Treaty enforced by peacekeepers sent by EU leader keeps Jewish and Palestinian extremists apart (start of final seven years)

1 year

Joel   **Ezekiel**

| Joel's 1st swarm of "locusts" | asteroid's near-miss showers meteorites onto the invaders *(Jews see this as a miracle and immediately rebuild the Temple)* | 2nd seal: red horse signifying war | Israel is invaded by "Gog" from the north: but the invading army is destroyed in a single day by fire from heaven. 7 months is needed to bury the dead. And they stink. | 2 years |

asteroid now showers more meteorites & larger bolides

1st trumpet, 3rd seal, 2nd & 3rd trumpets, 4th seal, 4th & 5th trumpets, 5th seal, image of the beast (abomination of desolation) erected in the Jerusalem Temple.

3 years

Matt., Mk.

abomination of desolation in the Temple in Jerusalem

3½ erection of abomination of desolation

Joel's 2nd swarm of "locusts"?

Jews flee. The Jews are persecuted but are protected in the desert. 666 economics system, Christians persecuted.

G R E A T

T R I B U L A T I O N

4 years

5 years

Diagram 8 of 12

Luke

signs in sun, moon and stars

sun and moon dark, stars fall, angels gather the elect

6 years

7 years. Armageddon

which is in human hands—so that "unless the Lord had shortened those days, no life would have been saved" *(Mk. 13:20)*. That would explain how there could be "tribulation such as has not occurred since the beginning of the world until now, nor ever shall" *(Matt. 24:21)* and then *later* the greatest earthquake ever *(Rev. 16:18)*. They are two distinct types of disaster: the one nuclear, caused by nations, the other cosmic, in the hands of God.

Muslim Reaction

As to reaction in the Muslim world to the abomination of desolation, I quote just one of the *ahadith* (or sayings) attributed to Mohammed:

> The Dajjal *[devil, false messiah]* will come forth, and one of the Believers ... will say, "O people, this is the Dajjal whom the Prophet told us about".   *(See page 71 for fuller quotation and reference.)*

So it seems that Mohammed foresaw that there would be Muslims who would recognise the antichrist for what he is.

The World's Reaction

It appears, however, that most of Christendom, and most of Islam (who may see the EU leader as the world's *Mahdi* or Messiah) and most of the Hindus (who may see him as a re-incarnation of the god Vishnu: *Bhagavad-Gita IV, 5-8*) will combine in worshipping their new god and benefactor whose image looks down on Jerusalem and the human race from the pinnacle of the Temple. *Rev. 13:8* says that all of them, worldwide, will worship him. And, as the 666 economic system is adopted in Africa, and Australia, and round the world, he can say, "I am becoming the World Ruler."

The worst is yet to come

That asteroid is still up there, though it has temporarily gone away on its elongated elliptical orbit. There are still two more Seals to be opened in heaven, and two more Trumpets to be heard on the earth.

Come back, O asteroid, come back and bring our Redeemer.

Pause for Paul

We shall look at the remaining two Seals and Trumpets in Chapter 8, but before that, we need to look at something that Saint Paul said.

- - - - -

Chapter 7

Paul

So far, we have omitted Paul, the writer of most of the Epistles. Paul had a dramatic conversion which left him blind for three days *(Acts 9:9)* but later he seems to have had insights beyond those afforded to most Christians.

Just a moment, please!

Can I interrupt myself here to make a rather important point. *Paul* on the road to Damascus saw the light and heard the voice of Jesus *(Acts 9:3-5)*. *Daniel* was visited by the angel Gabriel *(Dan. 9:21)*. *Ezekiel* saw and heard a superhuman being *(Ezek. 1:1-3 etc.)* and so did *Isaiah (Is. 6:1-9 etc.)*. *Jeremiah* heard the word of the Lord *(Jer. 1:1-5)*. *Jesus* spoke as someone with authority *(Matt. 7:29)* for he had divine authority. John's *Revelation* is "the Revelation of Jesus Christ" *(Rev. 1:1; and see also Rev. 4:1-2)*. *Peter* (whom we shall see in a later chapter) was a companion of Jesus, travelling with him and listening to him for about three years or more. *All these* had the voice of heaven in their ears—and I have not. Not even a dream. I am a reporter of what these men have said, and an interpreter, and indeed a speculator. **Do not** regard me as anything more—even when what is forecast in this book comes to pass—just as you don't regard the weather forecaster as anything more than a forecaster when the weather forecast turns out to be right.

Paul's first letter to the Corinthian Christians

Now: back to Paul. Hear what he wrote to the Christians at Corinth in southern Greece:-

> Listen, I'll tell you a mystery. We shall not all sleep *[i.e. die]* but we shall all be changed—in a flash, in the twinkling of an eye, **at the last trumpet.** *(1 Cor. 15:51.)*

Paul wrote that message several years before John wrote down the book of *Revelation*, so Paul had not read what it says in *Revelation* about the seven trumpets, but he seems to have known it. How?

Paul was very intelligent and highly educated. So was he familiar with Old Testament scriptures such as *Jer. 4:19-24*, "I have heard the sound of the **trumpet** ... I looked at the mountains, and they were quaking", and *Zeph. 1:14-16*, "The great day of the Lord is near ... a day of darkness and gloom, a day of clouds and blackness, a day of **trumpet** and battle cry", and *Zech. 9:14*, "The Lord God will blow the **trumpet**, and will march in the storm winds of the south"? Yes, he *was* familiar with these verses! He was a Pharisee (a member of the religious party) and the Pharisees knew their scriptures. And *Acts 17:28* shows us Paul quoting Greek poets, so he may well have read Homer and been familiar with *The Iliad, xxi, 387-388*, "The gods clashed with a mighty din, and round about, the great heaven rang loud like a **trumpet**". So he *may* have cottoned on to the notion that cosmic upheaval might cause trumpet-like sounds. **But there is not enough in that to give him the idea of "rapture at the last trumpet" without inspiration.**

Paul's first letter to the Thessalonian Christians
In his first letter to the Christians at Thessalonika (known today as Salonika) in northern Greece, Paul said:-

> The Lord Himself will come down from heaven, with a shout, with the voice of the archangel, and with the trumpet of God: and the dead in Christ shall rise first; then we who are alive and remain will be caught up together with them in the clouds to meet the Lord in the air. (1 Thess. 4:16-17.)

In the *Vulgate* (the Latin Bible) the word for "we shall be caught up" is *rapiemur* (first person plural future passive of *rapio* ... *raptum*) which is where our word "raptured" comes from. The actual word "raptured" is not in the English translation, which says, "caught up". Another equally good translation is, "snatched away".

Timescale
We will add Paul's remarks to the next version of our "prophecies in parallel" diagram: but space is getting a bit tight, so Paul will go over into the right-hand column (the "Daniel" column) to leave room for two more long columns (to be added later) on the left of the diagram.

- - - - -

Chapter 8

Can it get any worse?

Is there a pause between the first five or six Trumpets and the remaining one or two? We need to remember that the asteroid would be on an elliptical orbit (like a ball on a piece of elastic) and so the first four or five or even six trumpet-events could all happen in a single week, and then the asteroid might retreat for hundreds of thousands of miles, only to be drawn back again by Earth's gravity from which it has not got the velocity to escape.

Woe: the sixth Trumpet

The sixth Trumpet heralds some preliminary moves for an invasion from the east. The atheistic government of China (which has escaped comparatively lightly in the disasters which have swept across the northern hemisphere) wants no god. And perhaps it also sees the opportunity at this moment for China to become the top nation, as Europe is reeling and the other great powers have been laid low.

Believing that power comes from force of arms and not from the supernatural, two hundred million militia prepare to march westward, from east of the River Euphrates which flows through Iraq, and will in due course kill one third of those still surviving in the human race. *(Rev. 9:15-16.)* So here we have a major war looming. This, the second woe, is perhaps Joel's third swarm of locusts.

The sixth Seal

The sixth Seal has an earthquake. It is a huge earthquake: the sun goes black and the full moon blood-red, the stars fall *[meteorites again?]* and the sky recedes like a scroll rolling up. *(Rev. 6:12-14.)* And Isaiah, too, says, "The sky will be rolled up like a scroll". *(Is. 34:4.)*

And there is a scientific explanation for that! If there is such an explosion on Earth that its force rips right out of the atmosphere into the stratosphere (as happened on Jupiter when the largest fragments of the comet Shoemaker-Levy 9 hit it) the atmosphere with its blue sky would be rolled back by the force of the explosion, revealing the blackness of space.

And every mountain and island will be moved out of their places. *(Rev. 6:14.)* So the whole surface of the planet has been jarred. Britain is not precisely where it previously was, and nor is Mount Everest. The world's leaders (and the rich) are in underground bunkers *(Rev. 6:15)*.

Woe: the seventh Trumpet

The last of the seven Trumpets is accompanied by an earthquake, and a great hail of stones. *(Rev. 11:19.)*

"The second woe is past *[the Asians are marching, though they are still east of the Euphrates]* behold **the third woe** is coming quickly". *(Rev. 11:14.)* The third woe is at the seventh Trumpet.

It may be that the sixth-seal and seventh-trumpet earthquakes are both the same earthquake.

And now remember Paul's words: "We shall all be changed—in a flash, in the twinkling of an eye, **at the last trumpet**". *(1 Cor. 15:51.)*

So is this the Rapture? Let us consider the world-situation—and then the scriptures. Note in the diagram on page 47 how Paul's "rapture at the last trumpet", Matthew and Mark's "gathering of the elect", *Revelation's* "seventh trumpet" and *Revelation's* "harvesting of the Earth" all come level with each other. The bits of the jig-saw puzzle fit together. And I have not had to squeeze or twist the diagram to achieve that result: all I have had to do is to assume that the Seals are being opened in heaven at the same time as trumpeting bolides are being hurled at Planet Earth.

Is this the Rapture? Let's look first at the world-situation!

Rev. 13:7 says, "It was given to him *[the beast]* to make war with the saints *and to overcome them.*" (There is a parallel to this in *Dan. 7:25* "He ... will wear down the saints of the Highest One, and they will be given into his hand for a time, times and half a time".) A day will come when the last Christian church has been closed down, the last Christian book has been withdrawn from sale, the last Christian has been silenced, the last person to be saved has been saved. The door of salvation has been finally closed: the unsaved have closed it. The world thinks that this is the moment of final extinction for that hated and despised old-fashioned Bible-punching Christianity.

Imagine the rejoicing. "We have finally permanently silenced the noise of those enemies of human unity and human rights—those traitors refusing to join in worshipping the Emperor, those politically incorrect reactionary hatemongers, those holier-than-thou bigots ramming their unwelcome ideas down our throats and always carping on and on with their outdated *Christian* views *[spit as you say it!]* on morals and judgment."

What exactly has happened to the poor impoverished persecuted and totally disorganised Christians (no longer referred to in scripture as "the Church" but only as "the saints"—individuals to be picked off one by one until there are none left) is unclear. But they are defeated:-

"They said their Jesus was still to come—well where is he? He has let them down, and at last the whole human race has seen that their religion was false and restrictive and was a means of manipulating people for centuries. Well, they will manipulate us no longer! Their saviour did not come. Ours is here now, and his Final Solution to get rid of these misfit heretics has succeeded! They are finished for ever! So we can *'cast their fetters off from us'* and take our freedom."

And *that*, as the death-blow to Christianity is about to be struck, is the moment of the Rapture, according to *Dan. 12:1* and *12:7.*

> *Dan. 12:1* There will be a time of distress such as never occurred since there was a nation until that time, and at that time your people, everyone who is found written in the book, will be rescued. ...

> *Dan. 12:7* ... as soon as they finish shattering the power of the holy people, all these events will be completed.

Is this the Rapture? Let's look at some more of the scriptures!

Look how the verses just quoted from *Daniel* are parallel to *Matt. 24:21* and *24:29-31* which we saw previously on page 8:-

> There will be great distress (or tribulation) unequalled from the beginning of the world until now—and never to be equalled again. (*Matt. 24:21*)

> *Immediately after* the tribulation of those days, the sun will be darkened, the moon will not give its light, the stars will fall, and the heavenly bodies will be shaken. *At that time* the sign of the Son of Man *[Jesus himself]* will appear in the sky, and all the nations of the earth will mourn. They will see the Son of Man coming on the clouds of the sky, with power and great glory, and he will send his angels with a loud **trumpet** call, and they will *gather his elect* from the four winds... (*Matt. 24:29-31.*)

Surely, *there's* the Rapture! Wasn't Jesus virtually *quoting* here from *Daniel?*

Who are "the holy people" in the verses from *Daniel* quoted above? One interpretation is that it is the Jews, having their great religious revival at that time.   But it is "everyone who is found written in the book".   *Rev. 20:12* refers to books, the record of every person's deeds, "and another book ... which is the book of life".   *Rev. 20:15* adds, "Anyone whose name was not found written in the book of life, was thrown into the lake of fire". This appears to be the book of all those trusting in Jesus to have their sins "passed over" through the final Passover Sacrifice of the Lamb of God at Calvary—the book which Paul refers to in *Phil. 4:3* when he talks about "my fellow-workers, whose names are in the book of life".   Therefore "the holy people" in *Dan. 12* applies to the Christians alive at the end of the great tribulation. (Conversely, "your people" is the phrase used for the Jews in *Dan. 9:24.*)

Putting scripture with scripture

We need to bring quite a number of scriptures together here.

We have seen (in this chapter) the sixth Seal with earthquake, its black sun, blood-red moon, falling stars and the sky receding like a scroll rolling up *(Rev. 6:12-14)*

and *Is. 34:4*, with the sky rolled up like a scroll

and the seventh (i.e. the last) Trumpet, accompanied by earthquake and great hail *(Rev. 11:19)*.

Add to these the words of Jesus in *Matt. 24:29-31* "Immediately after the tribulation of those days, the sun will be darkened, the moon will not give its light, the stars will fall, and the heavenly bodies will be shaken. *At that time* the Son of man will appear ... and he will send his angels with a loud trumpet call, and they shall gather his elect."

and Luke's version "There will be signs in the sun, moon and stars ... *And then* they will see the Son of Man coming. ... When these things begin to take place ... your redemption is drawing near." *(Luke 21:25-28.)*

Note the opening phrase of *Matt. 24:29* above, "Immediately after the tribulation". This is the end of the Tribulation—at least for the believers, who are about to be raptured. And for what happens after this, the keyword is no longer tribulation: the keyword is wrath.

An eighteenth-century slave-owner would sometimes beat his slave to make him behave. But if he persisted in misbehaving, his owner might eventually give up on trying to reform him, and beat him severely to punish him. Up to here, the cosmic onslaughts have been warnings.

Asteroid Theory | Revelation | Daniel (timescale)

1st seal: white horse: emergence of a great leader

Treaty enforced by peacekeepers sent by EU leader keeps Jewish and Palestinian extremists apart (start of final seven years)

1 year

Joel | | Ezekiel

Joel's 1st swarm of "locusts"

asteroid's near-miss showers meteorites onto the invaders *(Jews see this as a miracle and immediately rebuild the Temple)*

2nd seal: red horse signifying war

Israel is invaded by "Gog" from the north: but the invading army is destroyed in a single day by fire from heaven. 7 months is needed to bury the dead. And they stink.

2 years

asteroid now showers more meteorites & larger bolides

1st trumpet, 3rd seal, 2nd & 3rd trumpets, 4th seal, 4th & 5th trumpets, 5th seal, image of the beast (abomination of desolation) erected in the Jerusalem Temple. Jews flee. The Jews are persecuted but are protected in the desert. 666 economics system, Christians persecuted.

3 years

Matt., Mk.

abomination of desolation in the Temple in Jerusalem

3½ erection of abomination of desolation

Joel's 2nd swarm of "locusts"?

4 years

Diagram 9 of 12

*
another bolide

6th trumpet: * 200 million invaders are preparing to advance from the far east.

G R E A T
T R I B U L A T I O N

5 years

Joel's 3rd swarm of "locusts"?

*
Is. 34:4 sky rolled like a scroll

Rev. 14:15 earth harvested

*
further onslaught from the asteroid

6th seal: * earthquake, sky rolled like a scroll, sun dark, stars fall: 7th trumpet.

Luke

signs in sun, moon and stars

sun and moon dark, stars fall, angels gather the elect

6 yrs

*
Dan. 12:7

Paul

*
rapture at the last trumpet

Then 7th seal: * 7 bowls of divine wrath will follow.

7 years. Armageddon

Events moved so fast I had to make ten additions all at once. I have marked them with asteroids—sorry, asterisks—to make them stand out.

Now they become punishments. The planet is to be thrashed to within an inch of its life.

Don't forget that it appeared to the world that this moment was to be the moment of final permanent defeat for the hated despised Christians: we saw that *Dan. 12:1* says, "There will be a time of distress such as never occurred since there was a nation until that time, and *at that time* your people, everyone who is found written in the book, will be rescued".

And *Dan. 12:7* adds, "*As soon as they finish shattering the power of the holy people*, all these events will be completed".

God has delayed the end of the age of grace until the very last possible moment, to give maximum opportunity for salvation—but now there is no point in delaying any longer. "There will be no more delay!" *(Rev. 10:6.)*

This moment is also described in *Rev. 14:15*, where the reaper swings his sickle (his reaping-hook) and the harvest is reaped. (Reaping with scythes or sickles was the normal way of harvesting corn until the invention of modern agricultural machinery—but today instead of a team of reapers there is one farmworker driving a combine harvester!)

Three verses later, there is another reaping—of the grapes of wrath.

And yes I know that I have quoted *Rev. 6:12; 10:6; 11:19* and *14:15* in this section, as if they are all one event: and so I think they are. Read the book of *Revelation* like a newspaper: and see these as four reports of a single event seen from four points of view.

Abandon your preconceptions!
I am all too well aware that readers of this book, if they have been taught anything about the Rapture at all, will in most cases not have been taught that it comes at this point. Some will have been taught that it comes earlier, before the beginning of the final seven years; some will have been taught that it comes later, at the *end* of the seven years, and some will have been taught that there is no literal Rapture at all.

Put all these preconceptions out of your mind and consider the scriptures we have just seen. For convenience, they are set out again on the page opposite, with seven "combinations" (of underlinings, italics, underlined-italics, bold-print, bold-italics, bold-underlined and finally bold-underlined-italics!) used to link seven groups of keywords, and on the verses we have seen earlier in this book I have added the page-numbers so that you can refer back to them. These twelve scriptures: *what do they say?* Decide for yourself.

Decide for yourself: do the pieces of this jig-saw puzzle fit together?

(a) the sixth Seal with *earthquake*, black *sun*, blood-red moon, falling stars and the sky receding like a <u>scroll</u> rolling up, *(Rev. 6:12-14.)* (pages 43, 46)

(b) the sky rolled up like a <u>scroll</u>, *(Is. 34:4.)* (pages 43, 46)

(c) the seventh (i.e. the last) **Trumpet**, accompanied by *earthquake* and great hail, *(Rev. 11:19.)* (pages 44, 46)

(d) "*Immediately after the tribulation of those days*, the *sun* will be darkened, the moon will not give its light, the stars will fall, and the heavenly bodies will be shaken. *At that time* the **Son of Man** will appear ... and he will send his angels with a loud **trumpet** call, and they shall gather **his elect**." *(Matt. 24:29-31.)* (pages 8, 46)

(e) "*In those days, after that tribulation*, the *sun* will be darkened, and the moon will not give its light, and the stars will be falling from heaven, and the powers that are in the heavens will be shaken. And *then* they shall see the **Son of Man** coming in clouds with great power and glory. And then he will send forth the angels, and will gather together **his elect** from the four winds..." *(Mk. 13:24-27.)* (not previously quoted)

(f) "There will be signs in the *sun*, moon and stars ... *then* they will see the **Son of Man** coming. ... When these things begin to take place ... Your redemption is drawing near." *(Luke 21:25-28.)* (pages 11, 46)

(g) "There will be a time of distress such as never occurred since there was a nation until that time, and *at that time* your people, everyone who is found written in the book, will be rescued." *(Dan. 12:1.)* (pages 44, 48)

(h) "*As soon as they finish shattering the power of the holy people*, all these events will be completed." *(Dan. 12:7.)* (pages 44, 48)

(i) "There will be no more delay!" *(Rev. 10:6.)* (page 48)

(j) *the reaper* swings his sickle (his reaping-hook) and the harvest is reaped. *(Rev. 14:15.)* (Three verses later, there is another reaping: the reaping of the grapes of wrath.) (pages 46, 48)

(k) "Listen, I'll tell you a mystery. We shall not all sleep *[i.e. die]* but we will all be changed—in a flash, in the twinkling of an eye, **at the last trumpet**." *(1 Cor. 15:51.)* (page 41)

(l) "*The Lord Himself* will come down from heaven, with a shout, with the voice of the archangel, and with the **trumpet** of God: and the dead in Christ shall rise first; then we who are alive and remain will be caught up together with them in the clouds to meet the Lord in the air." *(1 Thess. 4:16-17.)* (page 42)

But whether you agree or not, stand firm in the faith

Remember *Matt. 24:13*, "The one who endures to the end is the one who shall be saved" and *Rev. 3:5*, "The one who overcomes ... I will not erase that one's name from the book of life".

You *can* be erased. Terrifying, isn't it? But the message is, stand firm, keep trusting, don't give up your faith. Paul says, in *Gal. 6:9*, "In due season we shall reap, if we faint not", after his more drastic verdict in *Gal. 5:4*, "You have been severed from Christ ... you have fallen from grace". And in *Col. 2:18*, "Do not let anyone ... disqualify you for the prize". But the problem in Galatia and Colossae was that *false doctrine* had crept into the Church. Falling into sin is something all Christians sometimes do, but giving up the faith is something we *must not* do.

I put it this way. I was sinking in the darkness in a sea of sin but **I have been saved**. I let the divine lifeboatman pull me into the lifeboat. I do not have to row the boat, and though I am sometimes blinded and knocked backwards by great waves of sin washing over me, **I am being saved** as long as I do not jump overboard. (My dearest friend who actually guided me to this lifeboat is nowhere to be seen. Is she struggling in the darkness at the bottom of the boat? Or has she ceased to believe in the lifeboatman and jumped overboard where she will be at the mercy of the waves which are dashing people—and a couple of boats—onto the merciless rocks? I don't know. All I can do is tell people to hold on. Now there is a cry for help and another poor half-drowned creature lets himself be dragged aboard. The joy on his face as he is rescued encourages us all. Yet his friends mock him and avoid us.) And when we reach the harbour (as I am told we shall) we **shall be saved**.

The seventh Trumpet, continued

All this is only one aspect of the seventh Trumpet events. As we see the world deciding to cast off the fetters of the Christians' God, this is a good moment for us to remember what *Ps. 2:2-5* says:

> The kings of the earth take their stand, and the rulers take counsel together, against the Lord and His Anointed, saying, "Let us tear their fetters off and throw off their ropes from binding us!" The One enthroned in heaven laughs: the Lord scoffs at them. **Then He will speak to them in His anger, and terrify them in His fury.**

Don't forget that there has been an earthquake and great hail, and if this earthquake is the same as the one described under the heading of the sixth Seal, it has been so violent that the map of the world needs amendment because all the mountains and islands have moved, and there has been such an explosion as to blow a black hole in the sky.

Psalm 18 is "interesting":-

> In my distress I called upon the Lord,
> And cried to my God for help.
> He heard my voice out of His temple,
> And my cry for help before Him came into His ears.
> Then the earth shook and quaked,
> The foundations of the mountains were trembling
> And were shaken, because He was angry.
> Smoke went up out of His nostrils,
> And fire from His mouth devoured;
> Coals were kindled by it.
> He bowed the heavens also, and came down
> With thick darkness under His feet.
> And He rode upon a cherub and flew,
> And He sped upon the wings of the wind.
> He made darkness His hiding place, His canopy around Him,
> Darkness of waters, thick clouds of the skies.
> From the brightness before Him passed His thick clouds,
> Hailstones and coals of fire.
> The Lord also thundered in the heavens,
> And the Most High uttered His voice,
> Hailstones and coals of fire.
> And He sent out His arrows, and scattered them,
> And lightning flashes in abundance, and routed them.
> Then the channels of water appeared,
> And the foundations of the world were laid bare
> At Your rebuke, O Lord,
> At the blast of the breath of Your nostrils.
> He sent from on high, He took me,
> He drew me out of many waters.
> He delivered me from my strong enemy,
> And from those who hated me, for they were too mighty for
> me.
> They confronted me in the day of my calamity,
> But the Lord was my stay...

(Ps. 18:6-18.)

David wrote that psalm after his deliverance from Saul. But surely, this is more than just a poeticised account of a local skirmish between two rival chieftains in the tenth century B.C.

The seventh Seal

So there is rejoicing in heaven. The ransomed saints have arrived. (We see them in *Rev. 15:2-4* singing a song of praise. See also *Rev. 7:9.*) Then the seventh Seal is opened, and there is silence in heaven for half an hour at what is now revealed: *Rev. 8:1*. Then (and some would say, then *immediately*, within a few hours or even minutes after the Rapture) there come the seven bowls of God's Wrath—but the Christians are not on Earth to experience them.

The nation of Israel—God's chosen people—has not been raptured, and the world's policy towards them is summed up in *Ps. 83:4,*

> Come, let us wipe them out as a nation, that the name of Israel be remembered no more!

But God has not forgotten them.

Although at the opening of the seventh Seal there is thirty minutes of silence in heaven, the ongoing cataclysm on Earth may be far from silent, because I suspect that the main body of that asteroid may now be orbiting so low (and getting lower) that the seventh Trumpet will be a mighty sound continuing unabated and reverberating round the world right up to the Final Impact of the asteroid at the seventh Bowl of Divine Wrath *(Rev. 16:17-18)* which will be described in our next chapter.

On page 37 we saw a mention of 1,260 days. *Dan. 12:11-12* says, "From the time that the regular sacrifice is abolished, and the abomination of desolation is set up, there will be 1,290 days. How blessed is he who keeps waiting and attains the 1,335 days!" At present, no-one knows what that means. It has been suggested to me that the Christians will have to endure for a full 1,260 days (in accordance with *Dan. 7:25*, which puts the Christians into the antichrist's hand for "a time, times and half a time") and that the Wrath of God is the period from the 1,260th to the 1,290th day. I have no idea whether this is correct.

- - - - -

Chapter 9

It gets worse! (for those left behind)

The antichrist is fuming. My moment of victory is ruined! They've gone! They were snatched out of my hand just at the very moment that it was closing round them!

Jesus came for them "like a thief in the night". The world was taken by surprise.

In Heaven

Rev. 19:9, "Blessed are those who are invited to the marriage supper of the Lamb" (the Lamb being Jesus, the Lamb of God).

And then back on Earth

Then—with the Christians gone—there come the seven Last Plagues or Bowls of Wrath. These will be described fairly briefly in this chapter: I hope no-one reading this book will be there to experience them.

God's warnings have finished. This is Wrath upon this planet where not one single human is willing to submit to the Almighty.

The first Bowl

Malignant skin-sores break out on the people with the mark who have worshipped the image of the beast. *(Rev. 16:2.)* (Skin-cancers? Or do they have acid-burns from nitric-acid rain produced by the asteroid-strike? Just a guess!)

The second and third Bowls

The second and third of the seven Last Plagues *(Rev. 16:3-4)* make the waters of first the sea and then the rivers into blood. Ancient Mayan, Babylonian and Egyptian sources *(and Exod. 7:20-21)* tell of such an occurrence, which may be caused by pigmentation or chemical reaction from dust falling from the asteroid. Anyway, every living thing in the sea dies.

The fourth and fifth Bowls

The fourth Plague (or Bowl) brings fierce scorching heat from the sun *(Rev. 16:8)* and "they cursed (or blasphemed) the name of God, who had control over these plagues, but they refused to repent and glorify him" *(Rev. 16:9)* and the fifth one *(Rev. 16:10)* brings darkness on the realm of the beast. These are cosmic phenomena. An asteroid-strike could produce a heat-flash felt around the world, followed by such pollution that the sun is blotted out and the raging heat drops to months-long cosmic winter. "They gnawed their tongues because of pain, and they blasphemed the God of heaven because of their pains and their sores, and they did not repent of their deeds." *(Rev. 16:10-11.)*

The sixth Bowl
This dries up the River Euphrates, leaving the way clear for those two hundred million militia to advance westwards from the east.

Dan. 11:40 says that at the end time, the "king of the south" will collide with the antichrist, and the "king of the north" will storm against him. *Rev. 16:14* says spirits of demons go out to the kings *[or leaders]* of the whole world, "to gather them together for the war of the great day of God, the Almighty". So it looks as if the two hundred million from the east, and the antichrist's troops from Europe, and forces from Egypt in the south in company with the Arabs and/or the Africans, and Russia's renewed military might from the north, and indeed armies from the whole world, are all mobilising for a great world war.

The demons' spirits gather them to a place called Armageddon. *(Rev. 16:16.)* It is probably the valley of Megiddo, about seventy-five miles north of Jerusalem—but such a vast number of troops will be enough to cover Israel from end to end.

Jesus will come "like a thief in the night", and the world will be taken unawares.

Two Second Comings?
Just a minute: haven't we just seen Him come already—to snatch up the Christians at the Rapture? Can there be *two* Second Comings? My answer to that is to ask when was the First Coming. Was it when Jesus came as a baby in Bethlehem? Or was it when He rode into Jerusalem on a donkey, proclaiming Himself to be the Messiah? Both of those events can be called the First Coming, and they were about thirty-three years apart. If two events thirty-three years apart can be the First Coming, I have no problem with two events a few days or weeks or months apart being the Second Coming.

The seventh Bowl

The seventh and last Plague or outpouring of Wrath is the greatest earthquake of all *(Rev. 16:18)* and "the cities of the nations collapsed". *(Rev. 16:19.)* This time the whole planet is shaken, with catastrophe on every continent. And they blasphemed God *(Rev. 16:21)*.

On page 44 we saw (at the sixth Seal) "Every mountain and island were moved out of their places" *(Rev. 6:14)* but here the description is of something much worse: "Every island fled away and the mountains could not be found" *(Rev. 16:20)*. Here is a major change of geography (as in *Ps. 46:2*, "though the Earth should change, and though the mountains be carried into the midst of the sea") and huge hailstones (or hail of stones) fell from the sky. This seems to be the final impact of the main body (or remaining fragments) of the asteroid. This is the big one. The planet receives the most massive wallop. (Where has the Matterhorn gone? And what's that new lump that looks a bit like the Matterhorn—is it a piece of Holland or is it the remains of London? Or has Britain gone to join Atlantis?) This is perhaps the "stone cut without hands" of *Dan. 2:34* which finally shatters the antichrist's empire.

> Behold, the Lord lays the earth waste, devastates it, distorts its surface, and scatters its inhabitants. ... The earth will be completely laid waste and completely despoiled. ... The earth is also polluted by its inhabitants ... therefore a curse devours the earth, and those who live in it are held guilty. Therefore, the inhabitants of the earth are burned, and few people are left. ... The earth is broken asunder, the earth is split through, the earth is shaken violently. The earth reels to and fro like a drunkard...
> *(Is. 24:1, 3, 5-6, 19-20.)*

> The Lord will come in fire, and His chariots like the whirlwind...
> *(Is. 66:15.)*

We are told that Jerusalem will be pushed up to a greater height *(Is. 2:2; Mic. 4:1; Zech. 14:10)* and that there will be survivors in Jerusalem *(Is. 37:32)* and that there will be some survivors—although only a few—in other nations *(Zech. 14:16; Is. 24:6)*. There is terrific seismic activity in the Jerusalem region at this time, as will be noted in our next section.

And *still* the humans are at war with each other.

Jerusalem

About half a mile east of Jerusalem is the Mount of Olives, and between the Mount of Olives and the eastern rampart of the Temple Mount there is a deep valley. That is the valley of Jehoshaphat. *Joel 3:1-2* says, "At that time when I restore the fortunes of Judah and Jerusalem, I will gather all the nations, and bring them down to the valley of Jehoshaphat". (This is prior to the battle of Armageddon.) "Multitudes, multitudes in the valley of decision", says *Joel 3:14.* This is the fourth of Joel's four swarms of "locusts".

Zechariah says *(Zech. 14:2-5)* "I will gather all the nations to Jerusalem to fight against it; the city will be captured ... half the city will go into exile, but the rest of the people will not be taken from the city. Then the Lord will go out and fight against those nations, as he fights in the day of battle. On that day his feet will stand on the Mount of Olives, and" *[here comes the seismic shock]* "the Mount of Olives will be split in two from east to west, forming a great valley ... and you will flee by my mountain valley."

"They will look on Me whom they have pierced" *(Zech. 12:10)*—and so *at last* Israel will have recognised that the one their ancestors crucified, with nails piercing His hands and feet, is **the Messiah**.

Continuing Zechariah's prophecy *(Zech. 14:5-6)* "You will flee by my mountain valley ... then the Lord my God will come" *[says Zechariah]* "and all the holy ones with him. On that day there will be no light, the luminaries will dwindle." *[The Hebrew text is unclear: it could mean no cold or frost—but I think it unlikely.]* "It will be a unique day, without daytime or nighttime." That sounds to me like the main body of the asteroid has just fallen.

> The multitude of your enemies *[Israel's enemies]* shall become like fine dust, and the multitude of the ruthless ones like the chaff which blows away; and it shall happen instantly, suddenly. From the Lord of hosts you will be punished with thunder and earthquake and loud noise, whirlwind and tempest and the flame of a consuming fire. And the multitude of all the nations who wage war against Ariel *[Jerusalem]* even all who wage war against her and her stronghold, and who distress her, shall be like a dream...   (*Is. 29:5-7.*)

Zech. 14:12 adds, "This is the plague with which the Lord will strike all the nations that fought against Jerusalem: their flesh will rot while they are still standing on their feet, their eyes will rot in their sockets, and their tongues will rot in their mouths". And (*Zech. 14:15*) the same plague for their animals. These symptoms are those of nuclear radiation.

The scene moves to Armageddon.

Asteroid Theory	Revelation		Daniel *(timescale)*
	1st seal: white horse: emergence of a great leader		Treaty enforced by peacekeepers sent by EU leader keeps Jewish and Palestinian extremists apart (start of final seven years)
			1 year

Joel

Ezekiel

Asteroid Theory	Revelation	Ezekiel	Daniel
Joel's 1st swarm of "locusts" — asteroid's near-miss showers meteorites onto the invaders *(Jews see this as a miracle and immediately rebuild the Temple)*	2nd seal: red horse signifying war	Israel is invaded by "Gog" from the north: but the invading army is destroyed in a single day by fire from heaven. 7 months is needed to bury the dead. And they stink.	2 years
asteroid now showers more meteorites & larger bolides	1st trumpet, 3rd seal, 2nd & 3rd trumpets, 4th seal, 4th & 5th trumpets, 5th seal, image of the beast (abomination of desolation) erected in the Jerusalem Temple. Jews flee. The Jews are persecuted but are protected in the desert. 666 economics system, Christians persecuted.	**Matt., Mk.** abomination of desolation in the Temple in Jerusalem	3 years

Matt., Mk.

Asteroid Theory	Revelation	Matt., Mk.	Daniel
Joel's 2nd swarm of "locusts"?		G R E A T	3½ erection of abomination of desolation
			4 years
another bolide	6th trumpet: 200 million invaders are preparing to advance from the far east.	T R I B U L A T I O N	5 years
Joel's 3rd swarm of "locusts"?			

Is. 34:4	Asteroid Theory	Revelation	Luke	Matt., Mk.	Daniel	Paul
sky rolled like a scroll	*Rev. 14:15* earth harvested.	6th seal: earthquake, sky rolled like a scroll, sun dark, stars fall: 7th trumpet & the rapture.	signs in sun, moon and stars	sun and moon dark, stars fall, angels gather the elect	6 yrs *Dan. 12:7*	rapture at the last trumpet
	Joel's 4th swarm of "locusts", all nations against Jerusalem.	further onslaught from the asteroid; devastation; the greatest earthquake ever as it finally crashes into the planet.	Then 7th seal with 7 bowls of divine wrath, but in heaven the marriage-supper of the Lamb. Then Jesus returns in glory; Armageddon; Satan is bound and the millennium (1,000 years of peace) begins.		7 years. Armageddon	

Diagram 10 of 12

Armageddon

For the second time in this book, we see a leader coming on a white horse. The first one (page 22) turned out to be the antichrist, but the one now riding the horse is Jesus the real Christ. He comes with the armies of heaven. *(Rev. 19:11-14.)* The armies of the world are assembled against Him. No longer fighting each other, they have combined against their mutual enemy.

And there is a huge wave of water. *Dan. 9:26* which we saw on page 2 says the end will come with a flood. Habakkuk got the picture. What he says in *Hab. 3:10* appears in various translations as "Torrents of water swept by", "The overflowing of the water passed by", "The tempest of waters passed by", "The raging waters swept on", "A torrent of water streams by", "The downpour of waters swept by", and "Great floods sweep on their way". It is a vivid picture of an overwhelming wave of the sea passing over the land. He continues, "The deep roared and lifted its waves on high", or "The deep thunders forth, as it raises enormous waves". (Don't worry about the variations of tense here. It's a translation-problem. In Hebrew grammar, the tenses divide into "completed and uncompleted", and not "past, present and future".)

These prophecies tie in with *Luke 21:25* "And there will be signs in sun and moon and stars, and upon the Earth dismay among nations, in perplexity at the roaring of the sea and the waves". They tie in also with David Levy's description on page 227 of his book *Comets* in which he pictures a tidal wave five hundred feet (more than 150 metres) in height, wiping out coastal cities, with temperatures reaching 250° Fahrenheit (120° Celsius: it's above boiling point) after the crash of a comet into the Atlantic. Levy is not just a storyteller. He was a member of the astronomy team that discovered the Shoemaker-Levy 9 comet and watched what it did to Jupiter. (Look also at *Is. 28:17-19*.)

What all this suggests to me is a terrifying uplifting of the waters of the ocean resulting in a vast *tsunami* roaring unchecked across countries and carrying all before it...

The end of war

The beast and the false prophet (the second beast, the one that we saw on page 36) are captured and thrown alive into fire and brimstone. The rest of the troops are killed. (Drowned in the overwhelming flood?)

The demise of the beast (the antichrist, Satan's human body) leaves Satan as a disembodied spirit. In this form he is captured and is thrown into the abyss (the "bottomless pit") to be imprisoned there for a thousand years. *(Rev. 20:1-3.)* With Satan imprisoned, a thousand years of peace will now follow, with "swords beaten into ploughshares" *(Is. 2:4)* and Jesus ruling on Earth "with a rod of iron" *(Rev.19:15)*. Here begins the millennium.

The millennium

At the seventh Bowl, there was the final crash of the asteroid into this planet. Most of the asteroid will have been shattered and vaporised by the impact, though part of it may have gone right down into the Earth's core, and some shattered fragments have probably gone flying off into the depths of space. But the asteroid *has gone*. There will be no more disruption.

For the survivors of all this cataclysm, the process of rebuilding this wrecked planet now begins, at the commencement of the thousand years of peace of the millennium which Jesus and his saints will impose. Growing food in order to survive will be a top priority ("Fashion those weapons into ploughshares: that's an order!") and after that, re-drawing the Atlas of the World will be one of the first essentials. And now, the six provisions in *Dan. 9:24* (an end of sin, etc.) can at last be fulfilled.

Past, past, future

"These nations shall serve the king of Babylon seventy years." *(Jer. 25:11.)* "When seventy years have been completed for Babylon, I will visit you ... to bring you back to this place." *(Jer. 29:10.)* — *Fulfilled* after Nebuchadnezzar conquered Jerusalem *(literally)*

"A virgin shall conceive and bear a son" *(Is. 7:14.)* ... to be born in Bethlehem *(Micah 5:2.)* "and the Lord has laid on him the iniquity of us all". *(Is. 53:6.)* — *Fulfilled* in Jesus *(literally)*

"In a little while I will once more shake the heavens and the earth, the sea and the dry land..." *(Haggai 2:6.)* "This Jesus, who has been taken up from you into heaven, will come in just the same way as you have watched Him go into heaven." *(Acts 1:11.)* — *Remaining to be fulfilled* *(literally)*

In conclusion

This account has been brief. There has been no mention of the "little horn" from the Roman Empire in *Dan. 7*, which is the antichrist—not to be confused with the "little horn" from the Greek Empire in *Dan. 8*, which is Antiochus Epiphanes—and there is scarcely a mention of *Dan. 11*, though this will be considered (ever so briefly) on page 103. I have said nothing of Babylon, nor of the two "witnesses" who are prophesied to rise from the dead in Jerusalem—and one reason for not mentioning them is that I don't have all the answers. And there is no mention of Gaza, or the West Bank, or global warming, or court cases in the West on church-and-state matters, human rights (and duties?) etc.—and this is deliberate: these are all part of the big picture, but they are outside the scope of this book.

Stop press

As this book goes to the printers (at the end of November, 2006) the hostilities of the summer of 2006 between Hezbullah fighters and Israel, which devastated much of southern Lebanon, have been followed by a ceasefire for an indefinite period, enforced by UN peacekeepers from Ghana and other countries. (Ghana is of course not in the EU.)

As this *indefinite-length* ceasefire, enforced by *UN peacekeepers*, is not a peace treaty for a *definite seven years* enforced by *EU peacekeepers*, it does not fulfil the requirements of Gabriel's prophecy in *Dan. 9:27* (for the beginning of the final "week") which we saw on pages 2-4 above. The fateful final seven years is not upon us *yet*.

- - - - -

space for future developments

.

.

.

.

.

.

.

We must wait until Chapter 12 to read what happens at the end of the millennium. We are now going to go exploring upon a different track altogether.

Chapter 10

Islamic Prophecy: "the Last Hour"

The first question is whether this chapter should be in this book at all. Christians will not accept these prophecies as God's Word, but a billion Muslims would, and therefore Christians should not remain in ignorance of them. Christians: please read this chapter for information, just like the Prime Minister would read an opposition party's election manifesto.

Islam says Jesus will return
Islam teaches that there is one God. It does not accept that Jesus is divine, though it *does* accept him as a prophet.

Islam teaches that Jesus will return. This teaching is based on two verses of the Qur'an. In *Sura 19:33*, it states that the baby Jesus, speaking from his cradle, said, "Peace be upon me the day I was born, and the day I die and the day I am raised up again alive". (A similar story is in *1 Infancy 1:2-3* in the New Testament apocrypha.) *Secondly, Sura 4:157* says, speaking of Jesus, "They did not kill him and they did not crucify him but it was made to seem so to them. ... But they certainly did not kill him. Allah raised him up to Himself."

Therefore, if he has never died, he must come again—to die—in order to fulfil the prophecy that he gave from his cradle. The majority of Muslims therefore believe that Jesus will return, and will become a Muslim, and will die.

The Qur'an
To Muslims, the Qur'an is the Word of God, given to Mohammed through the angel Jibril (Gabriel).

Among non-Muslims, there are various views of the Qur'an. There are extremists who would swear that the whole book was inspired by Satan. Other views are that Mohammed made it up, from dreams and imaginings and from what he had heard from Christians and Jews; or alternatively Mohammed genuinely received knowledge from the supernatural but he accepted messages from bad spirits as well as good ones and so the Qur'an is a mixture of truth and error. Among Muslims themselves, some believe that on one occasion Mohammed was deceived and wrote some "satanic verses" which do not now appear in the Qur'an.

Some non-Muslims would allege that the Qur'an contains far more verses in this category than the Muslims realise. Then they might go on to point out that forgers (e.g. of dollar bills or other banknotes) do not try to make their work look *different*, but try to make it so similar to the real thing that people cannot spot the difference. And another view is that no-one can tell whether the Qur'an, or the Bible for that matter, can be regarded as genuine or not, and everyone is entitled to his or her own opinion. So the main alternative views about the Qur'an are:-

(1)   the Qur'an is the Word of God,
(2)   the Qur'an is the work of Satan,
(3)   the Qur'an is only a product of Mohammed's imagination,
(4)   the Qur'an is a mixture of (1) and (2), or possibly (1) (2) and (3)
(5)   we just don't know.

Many of those who go for alternative (2) (3) or (4) would go on to argue that as long as Satan, the master forger, can put over the message that we should *not* pin our faith on Jesus as our Saviour (because there is no such thing as original sin, and Jesus is not God nor the Son of God, and he did not die on the cross...)—as long as Satan can put *this* message over, he is quite happy for the rest of the message to contain some pretty accurate true prophecy (but even in the true prophecy, he could throw in some nuggets of misinformation to confuse everything).

Those are non-Muslim views, with which it was essential for me to start (to clear them out of the way) because for the rest of this chapter I shall try to give the Muslim beliefs and points of view.

I must leave my readers to make up their own minds as to which view they take. But the Qur'an looks to me like something more than the product of Mohammed's imagination. Decide for yourself whether it was *really* nothing more than his imagination which caused him to say,

> The Hour *[i.e. the end time]* will not come until the following events
> have come to pass: two big groups will fight one another, and there
> will be many casualties: they will both be following the same religious
> teaching ... people will compete with one another in constructing
> tall buildings...   *(see page 63 for the source of this quotation)*

Sources of Islamic prophecies
The prophecies come from two sources, the Qur'an and the Ahadith. (The Ahadith are the sayings of Mohammed. The singular is Hadith, the plural Ahadith.) Muslims see the Qur'an as the Word of God—and they

accept it far more literally than some people in Christian churches accept the Bible. The Ahadith, on the other hand, are the sayings of Mohammed—inspired, say the Muslims, but nevertheless the words of a prophet and not the Word of God.

Collections of Ahadith
In the early years of Islam after Mohammed's death (which was in 632 A.D.) great pains were taken to collect and record, as accurately as possible, his sayings, which at first had been passed on by word of mouth. The two most-highly-regarded collections of his sayings are those made by al-Bukhari (born 810 A.D.) and by Imam Muslim (born about 817 A.D.). Collections made by al-Tirmidhi, ibn Majah, al-Nasai and abu Da'ud (or abu Dawud) are also highly respected. An earlier very large collection, Ahmad's *Musnad* (the word means collection) is regarded as including some doubtful and even forged Ahadith.

Having a Muslim scholar named Muslim can be confusing. Where necessary, I shall use the adjective "Islamic" to avoid such awkward expressions as "the Muslim scholar Muslim".

A word about spelling
English spellings of Arabic names, and of Arabic words in general, can vary because of transliteration problems. Sounds of letters in the Arabic alphabet are not always equivalent to those of our ABC alphabet. There is also "assimilation", by which "al" before certain letters is assimilated to the letter after it. Thus al-Nasai can be assimilated to become an-Nasai, and al-Tirmidhi can become at-Tirmidhi: but the rule does not apply before an "F" or a "B", so al-Bukhari remains al-Bukhari, and his book *Kitab al-Fitan* ("Book of Afflictions") remains *Kitab al-Fitan*.

Isnad
An *isnad* (a chain of relation back to Mohammed) is always looked for. For example, the Hadith which we saw on page 62,

> The Hour will not come until the following events have come to pass: two big groups will fight one another, and there will be many casualties: they will both be following the same religious teaching ... people will compete with one another in constructing tall buildings...

is recorded by al-Bukhari *(Kitab al-Fitan, 9:237)* to whom it was handed down in a known chain of transmission from abu Hurayra who heard it from Mohammed.

This abu Hurayra followed Mohammed around and remembered more than five thousand things that he had said, but is regarded as having been sometimes none too perceptive. It is recorded that he said that "The woman who did not feed her cat will go to hell"—but Mohammed's wife 'A'isha (who appears to have been an extremely intelligent woman) pointed out that abu Hurayra had come into the room in mid-sentence, and that what Mohammed had said was that the woman who did not feed her cat was an unbeliever, and *therefore* the woman who did not feed her cat would go to hell. "Did not feed her cat" was said merely to identify the woman—it was not the reason for her going to hell!

Referencing

I have difficulty with Islamic referencing systems. The references I quote are those from the editions of al-Bukhari, Muslim and abu Dawud listed in the Bibliography at the end of this book. The collection by Muslim (published in English in four volumes) consists of 43 "books" (numbered 1-41, with two unnumbered) but quite independently it is divided into chapters numbered 1-1243, and the individual Ahadith are also numbered, 1-7190, all the numbers beginning from page 1 of Book 1. Similarly abu Dawud (English translation in three volumes) has books 1-36, chapters 1-1890 and Ahadith 1-5254, all numbered from page 1 of his Book 1. But al-Bukhari (English and Arabic parallel text in nine volumes) is more complicated. He has 93 books, with chapters numbered from 1 upwards from the beginning of each of the *books*, and the Ahadith are numbered from 1 upwards from the beginning of each of the nine *volumes*. Thus the Hadith quoted above as *9:237* is the 237th. Hadith in Volume 9. And there is a further complication: this reference, which is correct in the full version of al-Bukhari, is *2198* in the one-volume Summarised al-Bukhari in which the Ahadith are on a numbering-system from 1 to 2230 which is not in the full version by the same translator but a different publisher! Both versions agree that this is in *Kitab al-Fitan*, which is Book 88 in the full version but Book 84 in the summary.

In this chapter I give the number of the Hadith in the case of Muslim and abu Dawud, and the volume-and-Hadith number in al-Bukhari's case. I also give in all cases the name of the book (i.e. *Kitab al-Fitan* or whatever) which should be sufficient to enable a diligent researcher to find the reference even in an edition with a different numbering system.

The collections by at-Tirmidhi, an-Nasai, ibn Majah and Ahmad have not been available to me, and where I have quoted them I am relying on second-hand information from other authors, which may not always be accurate.

Kitab al-Fitan is also the name of Muslim's Book 39, and also abu Dawud's Book 30. One of ibn Majah's books, too, is *Kitab al-Fitan*. So, in the same way that I have in my bookcase several different books of *Poems by Coleridge*, by several different compilers, we have at least four books of Mohammed's sayings entitled *Kitab al-Fitan*, collected by four different compilers. (Muslim's translator translates *Kitab al-Fitan* as "Book pertaining to the Turmoil and Portents of the Last Hour", al-Bukhari's translator calls it "The Book of Afflictions", and abu Dawud's translator says, "Book of Trials", but the Arabic name of all of them is كِتَاب الْفِتَنْ *Kitab al-Fitan*.)

Classifications of Ahadith

Ahadith can be classified into *sahih* (sound) *hasan* (fair, reasonably reliable) and *da'if* (weak). There are also subdivisions: *gharib* (meaning rare) signifies a Hadith narrated by only one person, without corroboration, and a weak *maudu* Hadith is one which is believed to have been forged. On the other hand, *mautawatir* means that the Hadith was transmitted through the first three generations of Muslims by so many people that it must be genuine because it is not reasonable to suppose that such a large number of people might have agreed on a falsehood.

Prophecies

Now let us look at prophecies in the Qur'an and the Ahadith.

Gog and Magog

On page 22 of this book we saw Ezekiel's prophecy of an attack on Israel from the north, by "Gog from the land of Magog". This prophecy is in both the Qur'an and the Ahadith, though it is placed after the return of Jesus, whereas Ezekiel's prophecy seems to place it earlier. But compare this account with the one we saw on pages 22-24.

The account in the Qur'an says,

> But there is a ban on any population which We have destroyed: that they shall not return, until the **Gog and Magog** people are let through (their barrier), and they swiftly swarm from every hill. Then will the True Promise draw nigh (of fulfilment): then behold, the eyes of the Unbelievers will stare in horror. *(Sura 21:95-7.)*

The background to this is that *Sura 18:94-7* tells how Dhu'l Qarnayn (interpreted by some to mean Alexander the Great) filled a space between two mountainsides with molten iron and lead, so that the Gog and Magog people could not dig through it. They were thus prevented from doing mischief, but they will break out at the end time.

A footnote to Muslim *Kitab al-Fitan 6881* alleges that the barrier was built in a narrow defile between Derbend and Darial, in Daghistan. (Derbend and Daghistan are on the the western shore of the Caspian Sea. So the inference is that a barrier was built to keep the north-of-the-Caucasus hordes out of Alexander's empire. The Roman Emperor Hadrian did the same thing to keep the Scots at bay.)

The Ahadith give more detail of Gog and Magog:-

> Allah will send Christ *[sic]* son of Mary. He will descend at the white minaret on the eastern side of Damascus, wearing two garments lightly dyed with saffron, placing his hands on the wings of two Angels. ... He will then search for him *[Dajjal, the antichrist]* until he catches hold of him at the gate of Ludd *[Biblical Lydda, near Lod airport]* and kills him. Then a people whom Allah had protected will come to Jesus, son of Mary ... **and then Allah will send Gog and Magog** and they will swarm down from every slope. The first of them will pass the lake of Tiberias *[Sea of Galilee]* and drink out of it. And when the last of them passes, he will say, "There was once water there". Jesus and his companions will then be besieged. ... Allah's Apostle, Jesus, and his companions will cry to Allah, Who will send insects *[another translation says worms]* which will bite the people of Gog and Magog on their necks, so that in the morning they will all perish as one. Then Jesus and his Companions will come down and will not find any nook or cranny on earth which is free from their putrid **stench**. *(Muslim, Kitab al-Fitan, 7015.)*

> People will return to their lands and be met by Yajuj and Majuj *[Gog and Magog]*. When Yajuj and Majuj are let loose, whenever they come to water, they will drink it up. Whenever they come upon anything, they will seize it. People will seek refuge with Allah, and I will ask Allah to kill them and the earth will reek of their **stench**. *(ibn Majah, Kitab al-Fitan, 4081, 2/1365, 1366.)*

> They *[Gog and Magog]* will come out against people and drink all the water, and people will flee from them. They will shoot their arrows into the sky and they will come back blood-stained. They will say, "We have defeated the people of the earth and we are superior to those in heaven in strength and might". *(from abu Hurayra, narrated*

by at-Tirmidhi and by ibn Majah.   Another version of this, from a different source, is mentioned in Muslim, Kitab al-Fitan, 7016.)

So, just as *Ezek. 38:9* speaks of the northern invaders coming in such numbers that they are like "a cloud covering the land", so these Ahadith speak of them coming in such numbers that they drink the Sea of Galilee dry. The Ahadith agree with the Bible that the invaders will be suddenly destroyed, but whereas *Ezek. 38:22* (page 24 above) says the destruction is by fire from heaven, the Hadith says that insects (or worms) will bite their necks, "so that in the morning they will all perish as one".

There is a strange parallel here with the Old Testament account of the siege of Jerusalem by Sennacherib's army in 701 B.C. The Bible says *(2 Kings 19:35)* that 185,000 were killed in one night by "the angel of the Lord", whereas the Jewish historian Josephus says that the cause of death was a plague:

> God had sent a pestilential distemper upon his *[King Sennacherib's]* army; and on the very first night of the siege, a hundred and eighty five thousand, with their captains and generals, were destroyed. *(Josephus: Antiquities, 10:1:5.)*

So the Hadith 7015 is similar to what Josephus says, in that they both talk of some sort of a plague—but surely a plague would build up gradually: it would not strike down all the invaders in a single night.

So Islam agrees with the Bible that there will be an attack from "Gog" and that the attackers will be suddenly destroyed, but it disagrees with the Bible as to the timing of the attack and as to the manner of the attackers' destruction. And some people would ask whether Mohammed put this together from what he had heard from Christians about Sennacherib and Ezekiel and Revelation, or whether he had a more supernatural source.

Narrative of the "Last Hour"

A chain of "end time" events put together from various Ahadith reads like this *(the next twelve headings):-*

1. Mahdi

A *mahdi* or messiah will come:-

> The **Mahdi** will be of my *[Mohammed's]* family and will have a broad forehead and a hooked (or prominent) nose. He will fill the earth with

equity and justice as it was previously filled with oppression and tyranny, and he will rule for **seven years**.
(abu Dawud, Kitab al-Mahdi [Book of the Mahdi] 4272. Other versions say "seven or eight years".)

If there were only a single day of this world left, Allah would lengthen it ... until He sent a man from me or my family whose father's name is the same as my father's, who will fill the earth with equity and justice as it has been filled with oppression and tyranny.
(abu Dawud, Kitab al-Mahdi, 4269, with shorter version in 4270; narrated also by at-Tirmidhi.)

A nation which has me *[Mohammed]* at its beginning, 'Isa ibn Maryam *[Jesus]* at its end and the Mahdi in between shall never be destroyed.   *(Narrated by Ahmad and an-Nasai.)*

2. The time of Gog and Magog's appearance

The following Hadith of abu Dawud suggests that Gog and Magog are to be expected before the antichrist and the return of Jesus. This accords with what we have seen in previous chapters, but there is nothing to say that the ten events he mentions would occur in the order in which they are given: and we have seen on page 66 that Muslim puts Gog and Magog *after* the antichrist and Jesus.

The Last Hour will not come or happen until ten signs appear before it:

(1)   the rising of the sun in its place of setting,

(2)   the coming forth of the beast *(a footnote says this beast will come from the gap of the hill of al-Safa in Mecca)*

(3)   the coming forth of Gog and Magog,

(4)   the Dajjal (Antichrist)

(5)   (the descent of) Jesus son of Mary,

(6)   the smoke *(a footnote says this has been seen once before, in a famine in Mecca in which men were so pinched with hunger that they saw mist before their eyes when they looked up)*

(7-9)   three subsidences, one in the West, one in the East, and one in the Arabian peninsula, at the end of which

(10)   a fire will issue forth from the Yemen, from the lowest part of Aden, and will drive mankind to their place of assembly.
(abu Dawud, Kitab al-Malahim [Book of Battles] 4297.)

Quite apart from the Hadith 7015 narrated by Muslim which we saw on page 66 above, Muslim gives two versions of the "ten signs":-

It *[the Last Hour]* will not come until you see ten signs before and (in this connection) he made a mention of

(1)   the smoke, *[see also Sura 44:10-16 as to the smoke]*
(2)   Dajjal,
(3)   the beast,
(4)   the rising of the sun from the west,
(5)   the descent of Jesus son of Mary (Allah be pleased with him)
(6)   the Gog and Magog,
(7-9)   land-slidings in three places, one in the east, one in the west, and one in Arabia, at the end of which
(10)   fire would burn forth from the Yemen, and would drive people to the place of their assembly.

(Muslim, Kitab al-Fitan, 6931.)

The Last Hour would not come until the ten signs appear:
(1)   land-sliding in the east,
(2)   and land-sliding in the west,
(3)   and land-sliding in the peninsula of Arabia,
(4)   the smoke,
(5)   the Dajjal,
(6)   the beast of the earth,
(7)   Gog and Magog,
(8)   the rising of the sun from the west, and
(9)   the fire which would emit from the lower part of Aden.
(10)   was *either* the descent of Jesus Christ, son of Mary (peace be upon him) *or* the blowing of the violent gale which would drive the people to the ocean.

(Muslim, Kitab al-Fitan, 6932.)

The Last Hour would not come until a person would pass by a grave of another person and he would say: "I wish it had been my abode".   *(abu Hurayra, narrated by Muslim, Kitab al-Fitan, 6947.)*

There is also a version from al-Bukhari, part of which we have already seen on pages 62 and 63:

The Hour will not be established till:
(1)   two big groups fight each other whereupon there will be a great number of casualties on both sides and they will be following one and the same religious doctrine,
(2)   about thirty Dajjals (liars) appear, and each one of them will claim that he is Allah's Messenger,
(3)   the religious knowledge is taken away (by the death of religious scholars)
(4)   earthquakes will increase in number,
(5)   time will pass quickly,
(6)   *Al-Fitan* (trials and afflictions etc.) will appear,

(7)   *Al-Harj* (the killing) will increase,

(8)   wealth will be in abundance—so abundant that a wealthy person will worry lest nobody should accept his *Zakat* (charity) and whenever he will present it to someone, that person (to whom it will be offered) will say, "I am not in need of it",

(9)   the people compete with one another in constructing high buildings,

(10)   a man when passing by the grave of someone will say, "Would that I were in his place",

(11)   and the sun rises from the West.

So when the sun will rise and the people will see it (rising from the West) they will all believe (embrace Islam) but that will be the time when: (As Allah said,) "No good will it do to a person to believe then, if he (or she) believed not before, nor earned good (by performing deeds of righteousness) through his (or her) Faith". *(Sura 6:158.)* And the Hour will be established while two men are spreading a garment in front of them but they will not be able to sell it, nor fold it up; and the Hour will be established when a man has milked his she-camel and has taken away the milk but he will not be able to drink it; and the Hour will be established before a man repairing a tank (for his livestock) is able to water (his animals) in it; and the Hour will be established when a person has raised a morsel (of food) to his mouth but will not be able to eat it. *(al-Bukhari, Kitab al-Fitan, 9:237. From abu Hurayra. Also in Summarised al-Bukhari, 2198.)*

The first sign of the Last Hour, will be a fire that will drive people from the East to the West. *(al-Bukhari, Kitab al-Fitan, unnumbered Hadith between 9:233 and 9:234.)*

So we see that abu Dawud, Muslim (twice) and al-Bukhari have all recorded Mohammed's list of ten or more "signs". There are differences, giving the impression that these narrations cannot all be fully accurate: but remember that these compilers were working more than two hundred years after Mohammed's death. If several Christian compilers, working separately, were to make compilations of the sayings of John Wesley, whose death in 1791 was a little more than two hundred years ago, how much doubt and uncertainty over wording would arise? (The exception to this doubt-and-uncertainty factor is the Qur'an, which has been preserved in its original form more carefully than any book in the Bible.)

John Wesley was a preacher.   In that respect he was God's messenger, as are all preachers, including even myself: but none of us is God's Messenger in the way that Mohammed claimed to be.

There will be thirty liars among my *Ummah* (community). Each one will claim that he is Allah's prophet; but I am the last of the Prophets (Seal of the Prophets) and there will be no Prophet after me. *(Ahmad, Musnad, 5/46; abu Dawud, Kitab al-Fitan, 4239. A shorter version, not saying "last of the Prophets", is in Muslim, Kitab al-Fitan, 6988.)*

3. Oil wealth?

Soon the river Euphrates will disclose the treasure (the mountain) of gold, so whoever will be present at that time should not take anything of it. *(al-Bukhari, Kitab al-Fitan, 9:235 from abu Hurayra. Summarised al-Bukhari, 2197. Similar Ahadith in Muslim, Kitab al-Fitan, 6918-22 and in abu Dawud, Kitab al-Malahim, 4299-4300.)*

The Last Hour will not come before there is **much wealth** among you. It will overflow to the point the owner of wealth will be worried about who will accept his *Zakat* (charity) and until the person to whom he offers it says, "No, I have no need of it". *(abu Hurayra, narrated in al-Bukhari: paraphrased from Kitab al-Fitan, 9:237 seen on page 70.)*

4. Dajjal

The one that Christians refer to as the antichrist is referred to in several Ahadith as the Dajjal.

The Dajjal *[devil, false messiah]* will come forth, and one of the Believers ... will say, "O people, this is the Dajjal whom the Prophet told us about". ... The Dajjal will order that he be sawn in two from the parting of his hair to his legs, then he will walk between the two pieces. Then he will say, "Stand!" and the man will stand up. The Dajjal will say to him, "Don't you believe in me?" The Believer will reply, "It has only increased my understanding that you are the Dajjal". ... The Dajjal would try to catch hold of him so that he should kill him (again). The space between his neck and his collar bone would be turned into copper and he would find no means to kill him. So he will take the man by his arms and legs and throw him away; the people will believe he has been thrown into Hell, whereas in fact he will have been thrown into Paradise. *(Muslim, Kitab al-Fitan, 7019.)*

A shorter version of the same account, again narrated by Muslim, is,

He *[the Dajjal]* would come but would not be allowed to enter the mountain passes to Medina. So he will alight at some of the barren tracts near Medina, and a person who would be the best of men or from amongst the best of men would say to him: "I bear testimony to the fact that you are Dajjal about whom Allah's Messenger (may peace be upon him) had informed us". The Dajjal would say: "What is your opinion if I kill this (person), then I bring him back to life; even then will you harbour doubt in this matter?" They would say: "No". He would then kill (the man) and bring him back to life. When he would bring that person to life, he would say: "By Allah, I had no better proof of the fact (that you are a Dajjal) than at the present time (that you are actually so)". The Dajjal would then make an attempt to kill him (again) but he would not be able to do that.

(*Muslim, Kitab al-Fitan, 7017.*)

This Hadith *(sahih)* is corroborated by al-Bukhari:

Ad-Dajjal will come, and he will be forbidden to enter the mountain passes of Medina. He will encamp in one of the salt areas neighbouring Medina and there will appear to him a man who will be the best or one of the best of the people. He will say, "I testify that you are Ad-Dajjal whose story Allah's Apostle[pbuh] has told us". Ad-Dajjal will say (to his audience), "Look, if I kill this man and then give him life, will you have any doubt about my claim?" They will reply, "No". Then Ad-Dajjal will kill that man and then will make him alive. The man will say, "By Allah, now I recognise you more than ever!" Ad-Dajjal will then try to kill him (again) but he will not be given the power to do so.   (*al-Bukhari, Kitab al-Fitan, 9:246.*)

Ahadith *sahih* which are narrated by both al-Bukhari *and* Muslim are regarded as the most reliable that it is possible to have.

There would be no land which would not be covered by the Dajjal but Mecca and Medina, and there would be no passage out of the passages leading to them which would not be guarded by angels arranged in rows. Then he (the Dajjal) would appear in a barren place adjacent to Medina and it would rock three times *[i.e. three earthquakes would take place]* and every unbeliever and hypocrite would get out of it towards him.   (*Muslim, Kitab al-Fitan, 7032.*)

This too is a Hadith *sahih* and is corroborated by al-Bukhari:-

The terror caused by the Dajjal will not enter Medina. At that time it will have seven gates; there will be two angels at each gate (guarding them).   (*al-Bukhari, Kitab al-Fitan, 9:240.*)

There are angels at the mountain passes of Medina (so that) neither plague nor Ad-Dajjal can enter it.   (*abu Hurayra, narrated by al-Bukhari in Kitab al-Fitan, 9:247; with a similar Hadith in 9:248.*)

Ad-Dajjal will come and camp at a place close to Medina and then Medina will shake thrice whereupon every *Kafir* (disbeliever) and hypocrite will go out of Medina towards him.

> *(al-Bukhari, Kitab al-Fitan, 9:239.)*

5. Dajjal has only one eye

At least half a dozen Ahadith say the Dajjal will have only one eye.

> The antichrist is short, pigeon-toed (or bow-legged) woolly-haired (or curly-haired) one-eyed, an eye sightless, and neither protruding nor deep-seated. If you are confused about him, know that your Lord is not one-eyed.   *(abu Dawud, Kitab al-Malahim, 4306.)*

This description is reminiscent of the description of Saint Paul:

> Paul ... a man small of stature, with a bald head and crooked legs, in a good state of body, with eyebrows meeting and nose somewhat hooked, full of friendliness...   *(Acts of Paul and Thecla, 3.)*

That description is from the New Testament Apocrypha book of *The Acts of Paul*, in which it is reported that Thecla is converted through Paul's preaching and takes up a life of chastity, whereupon her fiancé stirs up the mob and gets Paul put in prison. Thecla visits him there, and is sentenced to death, but she and Paul escape to Antioch in Pisidia. Later she is thrown to the beasts in the Arena, but she falls into a tank of water and baptizes herself, the beasts are reluctant to pursue her, she is freed, and many people are converted as a result. And that is an early *Christian* document!

Let us look at some more references to the one-eyed Dajjal.

> (In a dream) I saw a reddish-white man with lank hair, and water dripping from his head. I asked, "Who is this?" They replied, "The son of Mary". Then I turned my face to see another man with a huge body, red complexion and curly hair and blind in one eye. His eye looked like a protruding-out grape. They said (to me), "He is Ad-Dajjal". *(al-Bukhari, Kitab al-Fitan, 9:242, see also al-Bukhari, Kitab at-Taghbeer [Book of Interpretation of Dreams] 9:128, 9:153.)*

> Allah is not one-eyed and behold that Dajjal is blind of the right eye and his eye would be like a floating grape.
> *(Muslim, Kitab al-Fitan, 7005. There is a similar Hadith in al-Bukhari, Kitab at-Tawhid [Book of Monotheism] 9:504.)*

> He *[Dajjal]* is blind in one eye, and your Lord is not so, and there will be written between his (Ad-Dajjal's) eyes the (word) *Kafir* (i.e. disbeliever).   *(al-Bukhari, Kitab al-Fitan, 9:245, see also 9:505.)*

> There would be written three letters كـفـر k f r (i.e. *Kafir*) between the eyes of the Dajjal.   *(Muslim, Kitab al-Fitan, 7008.)*

The inference is that he will have *Kafir*, unbeliever, written all over his face, rather like certain European leaders who made a point of omitting all mention of God from the European Constitution.

> Dajjal is blind of left eye with thick hair and there would be a garden and fire with him and his fire would be a garden and his garden would be fire. *(Muslim, Kitab al-Fitan, 7010.)*

The apparent discrepancy between Hadith 7005 (right eye) and 7010 (left eye) is explained by saying his left eye will be blind and his right eye will protrude like a grape. The reference to garden and fire is followed up in Ahadith 7011-7013, all of which speak of the Dajjal as having water that would burn like fire, and fire that would be like cold water. Hadith 7014 says he has images of Paradise (which would really be Hell-fire) and Hell-fire (which would actually be Paradise).

> Let him who hears of ad-Dajjal go far from him, for ... a man will come to him thinking that he is a believer and follow him, because of the confused ideas he awakens in him. *(abu Dawud, Kitab al-Malahim, 4305.)*

I had never come across any reference in the Old Testament to the antichrist being one-eyed: but then I found it. It is in *Zech. 11:16-17*, the prophecy of the Bad Shepherd. The prophet exclaims in *Zech. 11:17*, "May his arm be completely withered, his right eye totally blinded!"

6. Is the Dajjal a Jew?

> Ibn Sa'id said ... "What has gone wrong with you, O Companions of Muhammad, that you take me as Dajjal? Has Allah's Apostle (may peace be upon him) not said that he would be a Jew whereas I am a Muslim?" *(Muslim, Kitab al-Fitan, 6995.)*
>
> *[Ibn Sa'id said]* "Did Allah's Messenger (may peace be upon him) not say that he (Dajjal) would be a non-believer whereas I am a believer?" *(Muslim, Kitab al-Fitan, 6996.)*

I wonder whether there is a "blip" in translation in Hadith 6995, because we shall see on page 79 that some translators sometimes translate *Kafir* as meaning "Jew" instead of "unbeliever".

7. Constantinople captured?

> The Last Hour will not come before seventy thousand people of the descendants of Ishak *[descendants of Isaac, i.e. Jews]* attack it *[the city which has land on one side of it and sea on the other—i.e.*

Constantinople]. ... They will say, "There is no god but Allah and Allah is greatest" for the third time, and its gates will be opened for them and they will enter. They will be collecting spoils of war and distributing them when a cry will be heard: "The Dajjal has come!" They will leave everything there and turn to (confront) him.

(Muslim, Kitab al-Fitan, 6979.)

Here is a different version. One suggestion of its meaning is that the EU attacks Syria, but a Saudi army comes to their fellow-Muslims' aid. The hostilities lead on somehow to a capture of Constantinople (Istanbul)—but then the Dajjal comes. Another suggestion is that it refers to the crusades, and to the conquest of Constantinople in 1453.

The Last Hour will not come before the Romans land at al-A'maq or in Dabiq *[said to be locations in Syria near Aleppo]*. An army consisting of the best of the people on Earth at that time will come from Medina to oppose them. ... The Romans will say, "Do not stand between us and those who took prisoners from among us. Let us fight them." The Muslims will say, "No, by Allah, we shall never turn aside from you or from our brothers so that you may fight them!" They will then fight and a third of the combatants, whom Allah will never forgive, will be routed. Another third, consisting of excellent martyrs in Allah's eyes, will be killed. The last third ... will win and conquer Constantinople. While they are busy distributing the booty after hanging their swords from the olive trees, Shaytan *[Satan]* will call out: "The Dajjal has taken your place among your families!" They will then come out, but it will be of no avail, and when they reach Syria he will appear while they are still preparing themselves for battle, drawing up the ranks. The time of prayer will come and then 'Isa ibn Maryam will descend and lead them in prayer... *(Hadith Sahih, narrated by Muslim in Kitab al-Fitan, 6924, with a complete chain of authorities on the authority of abu Hurayra. Mentioned also very briefly by abu Dawud in Kitab al-Malahim, 4281.)*

The Dajjal will be followed by seventy thousand Jews of Asbahaan *[Isfahan in Iran]* wearing Persian shawls.

(Hadith Sahih: Muslim, Kitab al-Fitan, 7034.)

See next paragraph for continuation of the unfolding of these events:

8. 'Isa (Jesus)

Our next quotation is from the mediaeval Islamic scholar ibn Kathir, born in *c.*1300 A.D. Its source is unclear: he mentions ibn Majah, but this may be a compilation of various Ahadith from ibn Majah and others.

Whilst their Imam *[a righteous man; another translation says he is the Mahdi]* is going forward to lead the people in praying the Dawn Prayer, 'Isa ibn Maryam *[Jesus]* will descend. The Imam will step back so that 'Isa can go forward but he will place his hand between his shoulders and say to him, "You go forward. The *iqama [call for prayer]* was said for you". So their Imam will lead them in the prayer.

And afterwards Jesus will say, "Open the gate". The gate will be opened, and behind it will be the Dajjal and a thousand Jews, each of them bearing a sword and shield. When the Dajjal sees Jesus, he will begin to dissolve like salt in water, and will run away. Jesus will say, "You will remain alive until I strike you with my sword". He will catch up with him at the eastern gate of Ludd and will kill him.

The Jews will be defeated with the help of Allah. There will be no place for them to hide; they will not be able to hide behind any stone, wall, animal or tree—except the boxthorn *(al-Gharqarah)*—without it saying, "O Muslim servant of Allah! Here is a *Jew*, come and kill him!"

The time of the Dajjal will be forty years; one year like half a year, one year like a month, and one month like a week. The rest of his days will pass so quickly that if one of you were at one of the gates of Medina, he would not reach the other gate before evening fell. ...

Jesus son of Mary will be a just administrator and leader of my *ummah* (community). He will break the cross, kill the pigs, and abolish the *jizyah* (tax on non-Muslims). ... Mutual enmity and hatred will disappear. Every harmful animal will be made harmless, so that a small boy will be able to put his hand into a snake's mouth without being harmed, and a small girl will be able to make a lion run away from her, and a wolf will go among sheep as if he were a sheepdog. The earth will be filled with peace as a container is filled with water. People will be in complete agreement, and only Allah will be worshipped. Wars will cease. ... The earth will be like a silver basin, and will produce fruit so abundantly that a group of people will gather to eat a bunch of grapes or one pomegranate and will be satisfied. A bull will be worth so much money, but a horse will be worth only a few dirhams ... because it will never be ridden in war. *[He was asked: "Why will the bull be so expensive?"]* Because it will plough the earth.

For three years before the Dajjal comes, the people will suffer severe hunger. ... In the third year, Allah will order the sky to withhold all of its rain, and the earth to withhold all of its fruits, so that nothing green will grow. Every cloven-hoofed creature will die except for whatever Allah wills. *(ibn Majah, Kitab al-Fitan, 4077, 2:1363—and others?— as recorded in ibn Kathir page 58.)*

The son of Mary will kill the Dajjal at the gate of Ludd.
(at-Tirmidhi, Abwab al-Fitan, 2345, 6/513-4, ibn Kathir page 72.)

Muslim's description of the end times is one that we have seen in part already:

> He (the Dajjal) will be a young man with twisted, cropped hair, and a blind eye. ... He will appear on the way between Syria and Iraq and will spread mischief right and left. ... *[How long will he stay on earth?]* For forty days, one day like a year, one day like a month, one day like a week, and the rest of the days will be like your days. ... He will come to the people and invite them (to a wrong religion); they will affirm their faith in him and respond to him. He will then give a command to the sky: there will be rainfall upon the Earth and it will grow crops. ... He will then come to another people and invite them. But they will reject him so he will go away from them. They will have a drought and nothing will be left with them in the form of wealth. ... He will then call someone in the flush of youth, strike him with the sword, cut him in two pieces and (make these pieces lie at the distance which is generally) between the archer and his target. He will then call (that young man) and he will come forward laughing with his face gleaming (with happiness). It will be at this very time that Allah will send Christ, son of Mary.
>
> > *[At this point, Muslim gives the account of the return of Jesus and the coming of Gog and Magog that we have seen on page 66 above. I summarise it here.]*
> >
> > He *[Jesus]* will descend at the white minaret ... and search for Dajjal and kill him. ... Then Gog and Magog will swarm down ... and insects will attack their necks and they will perish as one single person ... and there will be no nook or cranny which is free from their putrid stench.
>
> Allah's Apostle, Jesus, and his companions will then beseech Allah Who will send birds whose necks will be like Bactrian camels, and they will carry them *[the rotting corpses]* away and throw them where Allah wills. Then Allah will send rain which no house of mud-bricks or (tent of) camel hair will keep out and it will wash the Earth until it resembles a mirror. Then the Earth will be told to bring forth its fruit and restore its blessing and, as a result thereof, there will grow (such a big) pomegranate that a group of people will be able to eat it and seek shelter under its skin, a dairy cow will give so much milk that a whole party will be able to drink it. The milking camel will give such (a large quantity of) milk that a whole tribe will be able to drink from it, and the milking-sheep will give so much milk that the whole

family will be able to drink from it. At that time Allah will send a **pleasant wind** which will soothe (people) even under their armpits. He will then take the life of every Muslim and only the wicked will survive, who will fornicate like asses, and the Last Hour will come to them. *(Muslim, Kitab al-Fitan, 7015. A very much shorter version of the first part of this Hadith, down to the death of the Dajjal, appears in abu Dawud, Kitab al-Malahim, 4307.)*

Observations: (1) Compare the rain washing the earth until it resembles a mirror, with the prophet Habakkuk's description of overflowing waters which we saw on page 58 above. (2) In the final sentence of the above Hadith, consider whether the reference to only wicked people being left is an attempt to describe the Rapture. (If it is, it is putting it very very late.)

The next Hadith is important for us to note, because it highlights a major difference (which we saw on page 76 but did not particularly note) between the teachings of Islam and those of premillennialist Christians.

The last hour will not come unless the Muslims will fight the Jews and would kill them until the Jews would hide behind a rock or a tree and it would say, "O Muslim! O Servant of Allah! There is a *Jew* behind me, come and kill him!" All the trees will do this except the box-thorn *(al-Gharqad)* because it is the tree of the Jews. *(abu Hurayra, narrated by Muslim in Kitab al-Fitan, 6985, with shorter versions in Muslim, Kitab al-Fitan, 6981-4. Also in Ahmad, Musnad, 2/417. See also the third paragraph of page 76 above.)*

Contrast this with God's prophecy spoken by Amos:

"I will plant Israel in their own land, never again to be uprooted from the land I have given them", says the Lord your God. *(Amos 9:15.)*

But teachers of "replacement theology" would say that such prophecies no longer apply to Israel: their belief is that such prophecies apply to the Church, which (they say) is the New Israel which has *replaced* Israel in God's Plan. So the premillennialists refer them to such prophecies as the following:-

I will bring them from the land of the north and gather them from the ends of the earth. *(Jeremiah 31:8.)*

and

I will take the Israelites out of the nations where they have gone. I will gather them from all around and bring them back into their own land. I will make them one nation in the land, on the mountains of

Israel. There will be one king over all of them and they will never again be two nations or be divided into two kingdoms. *(Ezek. 37:21-2.)* *(In Ezekiel's day, the nation had split into two kingdoms, Israel and Judah.)*

But when it is pointed out to teachers of "replacement theology" that after a delay of nineteen hundred years, these prophecies of the Jews' return to the land of Israel have largely been fulfilled within our own lifetimes, and are continuing to be fulfilled today, as we can see almost daily in television news programmes and documentaries, they reply, "Coincidence". They may be joined by preterists saying prophecy was for ancient times and not for today, and idealists saying the prophecies should only be taken symbolically, and "higher critics" saying that even if Ezekiel was not actually insane, we should not expect fulfilment of his (or anyone else's) ancient prophecies—the common factor of all these views being, "Don't expect prophecy to be fulfilled literally".

In the next Hadith we see what appears to be the same scene as in the last Hadith, but the word *Kafir* is used instead of the word *Jew:*

> On the night of the *Isra'* (Mohammed's night journey to heaven) I met my father Abraham, Moses and Jesus, and they discussed the Hour. ... Jesus ... said, No-one knows about its timing except Allah; what my Lord told me was that the Dajjal will appear, and when he sees me he will begin to melt like lead. Allah will destroy him when he sees me. The Muslims will fight against the *Kafirs*, and even the trees and rocks will say, "O Muslim, there is a *Kafir* hiding beneath me—come and kill him!" Allah will destroy the *Kafirs*, and the people will return to their own lands. Then **Gog and Magog** will appear from all directions, eating and drinking everything they find. The people will complain to me, so I will pray to Allah and He will destroy them, so that the earth will be filled with their **stench**. Allah will send rain which will wash their bodies into the sea. ... When that happens, the Hour will be very close, like a pregnant woman whose time is due, but her family do not know exactly when she will deliver.
> *(Ahmad, Musnad, 1/375; ibn Majah, Kitab al-Fitan, 4081, 2/1365-6.)*

And so, in the last two Ahadith, we have seen the persons taking refuge behind rocks and trees described both as *Kafirs* (meaning unbelievers) and as *Jews.* On page 76 we saw them described as *Jews.* And that is why I wonder whether, in the two Ahadith under the heading "Is the Dajjal a Jew?" on page 74, one person who heard Mohammed's words took *Kafir* to mean "unbeliever", and the other took it as an inference that "Jewish unbeliever" was what Mohammed really meant.

9. A millennium?

> Jesus (may peace be upon him) will soon descend (to the earth) ... wearing two light yellow garments, looking as if drops were falling down from his head though it will not be wet. ... He will break the cross, kill swine and abolish *jizyah* (tax on non-Muslims). All religions except Islam will perish. He will destroy the Antichrist and will live on the earth for forty years and then he will die. *(mautawatir: abu Hurayrah, narrated by abu Dawud in Kitab al-Malahim, 4310.)*

> The Last Hour will not come until 'Isa son of Maryam descends as a fair ruler and just Imam, breaks the crosses, kills the pigs, abolishes the *jizyah*, and is so lavish at distributing wealth that there is no-one to accept it. *(Ahmad and ibn Majah.)*

> The son of Mary will come down as a just leader. He will break the cross, and kill the pigs. Peace will prevail and people will use their swords as sickles. Every harmful beast will be made harmless; the sky will send down rain in abundance, and the earth will bring forth its blessings. A child will play with a fox and not come to any harm; a wolf will graze with sheep and a lion with cattle, without harming them. *(abu Hurayra, narrated by Ahmad in Musnad, 2/482-3, ibn Kathir page 74.)*

> Jesus will come as a just Judge. He will break the crosses and kill the pigs. *[Muslim scholars say that this Hadith means that he will judge according to Islamic Shari'a law.]* And then a boy will be able to put his hand in a snake's mouth, a girl will be able to make a lion run away, a wolf will graze with sheep and a lion with cattle, and the Earth will be filled with peace. *(Ahmad, Musnad, 1/375 and 2/482-3; ibn Majah, Kitab al-Fitan, 4077, 2/1363.)*

10. A rapture?

> The Dajjal will appear in my Community and he will remain for forty. *(Whether it means days, months or years is not specified.)* Allah will then send 'Isa ibn Maryam. He will seek out the Dajjal and kill him. Then people will live for seven years, during which time there will be no enmity between any two persons. After that Allah will send a **cold wind** from the direction of Syria. Anyone on the face of the earth who has a grain of good or faith in them will die. Even if some among you were to go inside a mountain, this wind would reach them and make them die. Only evil people will remain and they will be as

careless as birds with the characteristics of beasts. They will not recognise what is good or object to evil. Then Shaytan will come to them in human form and say: "Won't you respond?" They will reply, "What do you command us to do?" He will command them to worship idols and they will have abundant provision and comfortable lives. Then the **Trumpet** will be blown. ... The first one to hear it will be someone who is busy mending a cistern for watering his camels. He will faint and other people will also faint. Then Allah will send, or will cause to be sent, rain which will be like dew and from which the bodies of people will be re-formed. Then there will be **another blast** and they will stand up and look. Then it will be said, "O People, go to your Lord!" They will be made to stand there and they will be questioned. Then it will be said, "Bring out the party for the Fire!" It will be asked, "How many?" The reply will come, "Nine hundred and ninety-nine out of every thousand". *(Muslim, Kitab al-Fitan, 7023.)*

In this Hadith we see for the second time a reference to a wind (the first was on page 78) after which only the wicked are left behind—and we shall see it a third time in our next quotation which is from Mohammed's wife 'A'isha who remembered that her husband had said it.

He *[Allah]* will send a **sweet breeze** which will cause all who have the weight of a grain of mustard seed of belief in his heart to die; and the only people left will be those who have no good in them; and they will revert to the *deen [religion]* of their forefathers.

('A'isha, narrated by Muslim in Kitab al-Fitan, 6945.)

A time will soon come when ... only dregs of mankind survive... *(abu Dawud, Kitab al-Malahim, 4328.)*

11. After the rapture

(This next paragraph is a selection of Ahadith from various sources.)

When much wine is drunk; when men wear silk; when female singers and musical instruments become popular; when the last ones of this *Ummah* curse the first ones—then let them expect a red (or violent) wind, or the earth to swallow them, or to be transformed into animals. *(at-Tirmidhi, Abwab al-Fitan, 308; 6/4620-4658.)* ... People of my community will drink wine and call it something else; musical instruments will be played for them and singers will sing. Allah will cause the earth to swallow them up and will make apes and pigs of them. *(ibn Majah. And abu Dawud, Kitab al-Malahim, 4293, warns that this may occur in Basra in southern Iraq.)* ... Some will be swallowed up by the earth, some bombarded with stones, some transmogrified [i.e. turned into animals: cf. Sura 5:60 "Some He has

*changed into apes and pigs"; and Sura 7:166 "Be ye apes, despised
and rejected"].*　　　　　　*(Ahmad, Musnad, 2/163; also at-Tirmidhi.)*

Do not take that statement about transmogrification *too* literally—just
as when we refer to Jesus as the Lamb of God, we do not take the
phrase *too* literally, but mean he has the *status* of the sacrificial
lamb—not the wool and four legs of a lamb.

12. Mountains shall tumble and the trumpet shall sound

The Dajjal is not mentioned in the Qur'an—he is only in the
Ahadith—and so we have not seen much from the Qur'an in the last few
pages: but we need to end this survey with some verses from the Qur'an
that we can compare with the Bible prophecies that we saw on page 55.

> One Day We shall remove the mountains, and you will see the earth
> as a level stretch...　　　　　　　　　　　　　*(Sura 18:47.)*

> They ask you concerning the mountains: say, "My Lord will uproot
> them and scatter them as dust; He will leave them as plains smooth
> and level; nothing crooked or curved will you see in their place."
> 　　　　　　　　　　　　　　　　　　　　　*(Sura 20:105-7.)*

Sura 18, speaking of the day that the Gog and Magog people finally
break through their barrier, says,

> On that day We shall leave them to surge like waves on one
> another: the trumpet will be blown, and We shall collect them all
> together. And We shall present Hell that day for Unbelievers to see,
> all spread out.　　　　　　　　　　　　　　*(Sura 18:99-100.)*

The Qur'an appears to put Gog and Magog, the day of the trumpet
and the creation of new heaven and new earth, into one short period:

> But there is a ban on any population which We have destroyed: that
> they shall not return, until the Gog and Magog (people) are let through
> (their barrier), and they swiftly swarm from every hill. Then will the
> True Promise draw nigh (of fulfilment): then behold, the eyes of the
> Unbelievers will stare in horror:　...　Those for whom the Good
> (record) from Us has gone before, will be removed far therefrom. Not
> the slightest sound will they hear of Hell: what their souls desired, in
> that will they dwell. The Great Terror will bring them no grief: but
> the angels will meet them (with mutual greetings): "This is your
> Day—(the Day) that you were promised". The Day that We **roll up
> the heavens like a scroll** rolled up for books (completed)—even as
> We produced the first Creation, so shall We produce a new one.
> 　　　　　　　　　　　　　　　　　　*(Sura 21:95-7, 101-4.)*

Then when the Trumpet is blown ... then those whose balance (of good deeds) is heavy—they will attain salvation: but those whose balance is light, will be those who have lost their souls; in Hell will they abide. The Fire will burn their faces, and they will therein grin, with their lips displaced.   *(Sura 23:101-4.)*

And when the Word is fulfilled against them (the unjust), We shall produce from the earth a Beast to (face) them: he will speak to them, for that mankind did not believe with assurance in Our Signs. ... And the Day that the Trumpet will be sounded—then will be smitten with terror those who are in the heavens, and those who are on earth, except such as Allah will please (to exempt). ... You see the mountains and think them firmly fixed: but they shall pass away as the clouds pass away.   *(Sura 27:82, 87-8.)*

Verily, the knowledge of the Hour is with Allah (alone).
(Sura 31:34.)

The trumpet shall be sounded, when behold, from the sepulchres (men) will rush forth to their Lord!   *(Sura 36:51.)*

The Trumpet will (just) be sounded, when all that are in the heavens and on earth will swoon, except such as it will please Allah (to exempt). Then will a second one be sounded, when, behold, they will be standing and looking on! And the Earth will shine with the Glory of its Lord: the Record (of Deeds) will be placed (open); the prophets and the witnesses will be brought forward; and a just decision pronounced between them; and they will not be wronged (in the least). And to every soul will be paid in full (the fruit) of its Deeds; and (Allah) knows best all that they do. The Unbelievers will be led to Hell in crowds ... Enter the gates of Hell, to dwell therein ... And those who feared their Lord will be led to the Garden in crowds.
(Sura 39:68-73.)

The Day when the Earth will be rent asunder, from (men) hurrying out: that will be a gathering together—quite easy for Us.
(Sura 50:44.)

Verily, the Doom of thy Lord will indeed come to pass—there is none can avert it—on the Day when the Firmament will be in dreadful commotion and the mountains will fly hither and thither. ... (Those who believe will say:) "But Allah has been good to us, and has delivered us from the Penalty of the Scorching Wind".
(Sura 52:7-10 and 27.)

The Hour (of Judgment) is nigh, and the moon is cleft asunder.
(Sura 54:1.)

When the sky is rent asunder, and it becomes red like ointment: then which of the favours of your Lord will you deny? *(Sura 55:37-8.)*

When the earth shall be shaken to its depths, and the mountains shall be crumbled to atoms, becoming dust scattered abroad ...
(Sura 56:4-6.)

And We have, (from of old), adorned the lowest heaven with Lamps, and We have made such (lamps) (as) missiles to drive away the Evil Ones, *[or missiles to pelt the devils with, says another translator]* and have prepared for them the Penalty of the Blazing Fire. ... Do you feel secure that He Who is in heaven will not cause you to be swallowed up by the earth when it shakes (as in an earthquake)? Or do you feel secure that He Who is in heaven will not send against you a violent tornado (with showers of stones), so that you shall know how (terrible) was My warning?   *(Sura 67:5, 16-17.)*

One Day the earth and the mountains will be in violent commotion, and the mountains will be as a heap of sand poured out and flowing down. ... Then how shall you, if you deny (Allah), guard yourselves against a Day that will make children white-haired—whereon the sky will be cleft asunder?   *(Sura 73:14, 17-8.)*

At length, when the sight is dazed, and the moon is buried in darkness, and the sun and moon are joined together—That Day will Man say: "Where is the refuge?" By no means! No place of safety!
(Sura 75:7-11.)

Then when the stars become dim; when the heaven is cleft asunder; when the mountains are scattered (to the winds) as dust; and when the apostles are (all) appointed a time (to collect)—for what Day are these (Portents) deferred? For the day of Decision.   *(Sura 77:7-13.)*

The Day that the Trumpet shall be sounded, and you shall come forth in crowds; and the heavens shall be opened as if there were doors, and the mountains shall vanish, as if they were a mirage. ...
(Sura 78:18-20.)

At length, when there comes the Deafening Noise—that Day shall a man flee from his own brother, and from his mother and his father, and from his wife and his children.   *(Sura 80:33-4.)*

When the sun (with its spacious light) is folded up; when the stars fall, losing their lustre; when the mountains vanish (like a mirage); when the she-camels, ten months with young, are left, untended; when the wild beasts are herded together (in the human habitations); when the oceans boil over with a swell; ... when the Scrolls are laid open;

Islam	Asteroid Theory	Revelation		Daniel *(timescale)*
The *Mahdi* (a messiah) will come		1st seal: white horse: emergence of a great leader		Treaty enforced by peacekeepers sent by EU leader keeps Jewish and Palestinian extremists apart (start of final seven years)
				1 year

Joel | | | Ezekiel |

Joel				**Ezekiel**	
Joel's 1st swarm of "locusts"	"Gog & Magog" swarm down from the north *after* the return of Jesus, but are destroyed in a single night by insects or worms biting their necks, and they will stink.	asteroid's near-miss showers meteorites onto the invaders *(Jews see this as a miracle and immediately rebuild the Temple)*	2nd seal: red horse signifying war	Israel is invaded by "Gog" from the north: but the invading army is destroyed in a single day by fire from heaven. 7 months is needed to bury the dead. And they stink.	2 years
	The Dajjal (the antichrist) will come, but cannot enter the city of Medina.	asteroid now showers more meteorites & larger bolides	1st trumpet, 3rd seal, 2nd & 3rd trumpets, 4th seal, 4th & 5th trumpets, 5th seal, image of the beast (abomination of desolation) erected in the Jerusalem Temple. Jews flee.		3 years
				Matt., Mk.	
Joel's 2nd swarm of "locusts"?			The Jews are persecuted but are protected in the desert. 666 economics system, Christians persecuted.	abomination of desolation in the Temple in Jerusalem	3½ erection of abomination of desolation
				G R E A T	4 years

Diagram 11 of 12

				T R	
Joel's 3rd swarm of "locusts"?	The sun will rise from the west: a trumpet shall sound: the stars become dim, the moon dark and rent apart, the mountains are removed, and the heavens roll up like a scroll.	another bolide	6th trumpet: 200 million invaders are preparing to advance from the far east.	I B U L A T I	5 years
Is. 34:4 sky rolled like a scroll			6th seal: earthquake, sky rolled like a scroll, sun dark,	O N **Luke**	6 yrs
Rev. 14:15 earth harvested.	Jesus will kill the Dajjal, Allah will defeat the Jews. A time of plenty will come but then all good people will die & the End comes.	further onslaught from the asteroid; devastation; the greatest earthquake ever as it finally crashes into the planet.	stars fall; 7th trumpet & the rapture. Then 7th seal with 7 bowls of divine wrath, but in heaven the marriage-supper of the Lamb. Then Jesus returns in glory; Armageddon; Satan is bound and the millennium (1,000 years of peace) begins.	signs in sun, moon and stars	**Paul** rapture at the *Dan. 12:7* last trumpet
Joel's 4th swarm of "locusts", all nations against Jerusalem.				sun and moon dark, stars fall, angels gather the elect	7 years. Armageddon

Luke: signs in sun, moon and stars — sun and moon dark, stars fall, angels gather the elect

Paul: rapture at the last trumpet — *Dan. 12:7*

when the World on High is unveiled; when the Blazing Fire is kindled to fierce heat; and when the Garden is brought near, (then) shall each soul know what it has put forward.   *(Sura 81:1-6, 10-14.)*

When the Sky is cleft asunder; when the Stars are scattered; when the Oceans are suffered to burst forth; and when the Graves are turned upside down, (then) shall each soul know what it hath sent forward and (what it hath) kept back.   *(Sura 82:1-5.)*

When the Sky is rent asunder, and hearkens to (the Command of) its Lord ... and when the Earth is flattened out, and casts forth what is within it and becomes (clean) empty, and hearkens to (the Command of) its Lord ... (then will come home the full Reality). *(Sura 84:1-5.)*

When the Earth is shaken to her (utmost) convulsion, and throws up her burdens (from within), and man cries (distressed): "What is the matter with her?" On that day will she declare her tidings.
    (Sura 99:1-4.)

Then, he whose balance (of good deeds) will be (found) heavy, will be in a Life of good pleasure and satisfaction, but he whose balance (of good deeds) will be (found) light will have his home in a (bottomless) Pit. And what will explain to you what this is? (It is) a Fire blazing fiercely!   *(Sura 101:6-11.)*

The twentieth-century Islamic scholar Said-i Nursi has forecast that "Present Christianity will be purified ... it will cast off superstition and distortion, and unite with the truths of Islam". *(The Fifteenth Letter, 54.)*

To sum up
Do we find references in these Muslim prophecies to the final seven years, the attack on Israel from the north, the antichrist, the Rapture, the trumpets, movement of mountains, the millennium (or a period of peace) and an eventual new heaven and new earth? Yes, we do!

I must leave my readers to decide for themselves whether Mohammed was divinely or otherwise inspired or whether he formulated these ideas from what he had heard from Christians and Jews: but I personally cannot accept that what is in this chapter is the final Message of God superseding all previous scripture.

- - - - -

Now back to the Bible:-

Chapter 11

An intellectual look at *Daniel*

In Chapter 1 we applied the "futurist" view of *Dan. 9:24-27*. But actually there are three views:-

(a) the Maccabaean (or critical) view,
(b) the Messianic (or traditional) view, and
(c) the end-times (or futurist) view.

In a minute we will look at each of them.

Dan. 9:24 predicts seventy "weeks" (or seventy "sevens") and if a "week" means not seven days but seven years, seventy "weeks" is 490 years. Whether these are solar (365¼ day) years, or lunar (354 day) years, or ancient Babylonian (360 day) years, is much disputed. We shall encounter all three in this chapter: but assume in this chapter that solar (365¼ day) years are meant, except where otherwise stated.

Dan. 9:25 divides the seventy "weeks" or "sevens" (490 years) into seven "sevens" (49 years) plus sixty-two "sevens" (434 years) plus one "seven" (7 years). In Chapter 1 we added the seven "sevens" and the sixty-two "sevens" together to make sixty-nine "sevens" (483 years).

When did this period of 490 years start? We are told in *Dan. 9:25* that it starts from a command (or a "word") to rebuild Jerusalem. (Remember that in Daniel's time, Jerusalem and its Temple were in ruins. Nebuchadnezzar's army had burnt the Temple and the entire city in 586 B.C.) So when was this "word" to rebuild given? Half a dozen dates have been suggested. Most of them must be treated as give-or-take a year or two because of the uncertainty of ancient records and the variations of ancient calendars which did not have their New Year's Day when we have ours. For instance, the new year might begin on March 25th. as in the Julian calendar of Julius Caesar as used in Britain until 1752, or March/April varying according to the date of the new moon as in the Jewish religious calendar, or September as in the Jewish civil calendar. (Anyone who has spent their December-January Christmas holiday filling in a tax form for the British tax year running from April 5th. to April 4th., for an organisation with a September-to-September accounting year, will understand the nature of the problem!) Here are the main dates:-

1) **606 or 605 B.C.** This was the date that Nebuchadnezzar took Daniel and his friends into exile to Babylon, and the prophet Jeremiah gave the prophetic word—that Jerusalem would be totally destroyed—that we can read in *Jer. 25:9-12.* (Babylon was on the banks of the River Euphrates, about sixty miles south of Baghdad in what is now Iraq.)

2) **597 B.C.** was the date that Nebuchadnezzar took thousands of Jews into exile to Babylon, and Jeremiah wrote them a letter (which we can read in *Jer. 29:4-14)* saying that the desolation would last 70 years.

3) **586 B.C.** was the date that Nebuchadnezzar's troops burnt Jerusalem and the Temple, and took more Jews into exile. (The details are in *2 Kings 25:9,   2 Chron. 36:19* and *Jer. 52:13.)*

4) **538 B.C.** was the year when the Medo-Persian king Cyrus, who had just conquered Babylon, allowed the Jews to return to Jerusalem (though in fact only about 43,000 of them did so) to rebuild *the Temple. (Ezra 1:1-4.)* From here on, take note of whether the order is to rebuild *the Temple* or to rebuild *the city.* Gabriel's prophecy in *Dan. 9:25* speaks of 490 years from a command or a word to rebuild *the city.*

But some people claim that Cyrus' action indicates that a divine edict, that it was time to set in motion the process of rebuilding *Jerusalem,* had been spoken *in heaven.* (Another version surmises that such a heavenly command must have been made in 458 B.C. when King Artaxerxes made a decree which we shall see in a moment.) In other words, they "see" a divine command which is not in the Bible. (Isn't that cheating?)

5) **520 B.C.** is the date of an order by the king Darius Hystaspis confirming Cyrus' decree. (The details are in *Ezra 4:24* and *6:1-13.)*

6) **458 or 457 B.C.** (the seventh year of King Artaxerxes) is the date of Artaxerxes' order to Ezra (set out in full in *Ezra 7:11-26)* to support the Temple services and to enforce the Levitical Law (the Law of Moses) in Jerusalem.

7) **445 or 444 B.C.** (the twentieth year of King Artaxerxes) is the year when Artaxerxes gave Nehemiah permission (which amounted to a command—because Nehemiah might well have been executed if he had not obeyed it—and he knew it) to rebuild *the city of Jerusalem.* The details are in *Neh. 2:1-9.*

Now, keeping those dates in mind, let us look at the three views—the Maccabaean, the Messianic and the end-times views—but first, let us just remind ourselves of the gist of what Gabriel said:-

From a word to rebuild Jerusalem to an anointed one, a prince, shall be seven sevens: and sixty-two sevens: the city shall be rebuilt with streets and a trench (or moat): after the sixty-two sevens, an anointed one shall be cut off and shall have nothing. (The Hebrew for an "anointed one" is חישמ *meshiach*, often translated as Messiah.) The people of a prince who is to come will destroy Jerusalem and its Temple. He will make firm a covenant (or enforce a treaty) for one seven, but in the middle of the seven he will stop the sacrifices and erect the abomination of desolation (or, on the wing of abominations comes a desolator—the Hebrew is unclear here). But desolation will finally be poured out on the desolator (or on the desolate city).

(This is a summarised paraphrase. Check *Dan. 9:24-27* in your Bible to get the actual words: and see also page 2, above.)

The phrase "and a trench (or moat)" puzzles academics, but they should look in the British Museum, where there are two "barrel cylinders" on which Nebuchadnezzar boasts of his building works in and around Babylon, completing the city walls and improving and constructing a "quay and ditch (or moat)". (See Appendix 2 on page 118 for an extract.) Gabriel is probably having a dig at Nebuchadnezzar's great boast here, and is saying that Jerusalem will be rebuilt, as solid as that.

Now let us look at the three views.

(a) The Maccabaean (or Critical) View

From 586 B.C. (Jerusalem burnt) down to 537 B.C. (the Jews arriving back in ruined Jerusalem) is forty-nine years. *There* are the first seven "sevens". So the anointed one, the prince, coming at the end of the seven "sevens" must be Cyrus, the king who let the Jews return home in 538 B.C.

And the final "seven" is the seven years from 171 to 164 B.C. The prophecy says, "An anointed one shall be cut off"—and in 171 B.C. it happened: the deposed High Priest Onias III was murdered after he rebuked the current High Priest Menelaus (who was an apostate) for stealing golden goblets from the Temple. Then, in December of 168 B.C., the king Antiochus Epiphanes (trying to enforce the Greek religion across his empire) erected an altar to Jupiter on top of the Temple altar—an abomination of desolation—and the sacrifices were stopped for exactly (to the very day) three years. (He also sacrificed a pig, which the Jews see as an unclean animal, says Josephus: *Antiquities 12:5:4*.) The **Maccabees** revolted against his rule, and restored the Temple sacrifices in December of 165 B.C., and Antiochus Epiphanes died in 164 B.C. (The story is told in *1 Macc. 1:10 - 6:14* and *2 Macc. 3:1 - 10:9* in the Apocrypha.)

Here, it is claimed, is the final "week", the final seven years, from 171 to 164 B.C. During that period, an anointed one (Onias) was cut off, Antiochus Epiphanes may well have made a covenant with the apostate pro-Greek Jewish party, which was a powerful body, with Menelaus as one of its leaders—and in the middle of the "week", the sacrifices were stopped and the abomination of desolation was erected.

So the prophecy in *Dan. 9:24-27* is not a prophecy of the Messiah at all—it is about events which had all ended by 164 B.C.—and it probably isn't even a prophecy, but was probably written between 167 and 164 B.C. as a fable or pep-talk to encourage those who were rebelling against Antiochus Epiphanes. But even if there *was* an ancient prophecy, this fulfilled it—so, for us, all of this is just history.

In favour of this theory, it must be admitted that the references to the abomination of desolation in *Dan. 8:11-12* and *Dan. 11:31* really *do* appear to apply to the activities of Antiochus Epiphanes, though a "double fulfilment" (by Antiochus Epiphanes and also by the antichrist) is a strong possibility.

Problems with the Maccabaean View

But there are problems with this theory. For instance, it sees Antiochus Epiphanes as the prince who was to come, but, contrary to the prophecy, his troops *did not* destroy Jerusalem and the Temple. They carried out a massacre in Jerusalem, and polluted the Temple, but they did not destroy them. In this respect, the prophecy was *not fulfilled.*

Secondly, what about that sixty-two "sevens", which should amount to 434 years? (62 x 7 = 434.) We saw that the first seven "sevens" (forty-nine years) ended in 537 B.C. and that the final "seven" began in 171 B.C. So is it 434 years from 537 to 171 B.C.? Oh dear, it's only 366 years: it's *sixty-eight years short.* (An answer often given to this is that the Book of Daniel was written in about 165 B.C. by someone who did not have a perfect knowledge of ancient history and worked from an inaccurate set of dates.) But if you want the arithmetic to add up, the likeliest way I know of getting it even approximately right is to make the forty-nine years and the 434 years concurrent (running side by side) instead of consecutive (one after the other) so the forty-nine years *might* run from 586 to 537 B.C., but the 434 years must run from 605 (Jeremiah's prophecy in *Jer. 25:9-12*) to 171 B.C. But that prophecy of Jeremiah's said, "This whole country will become a desolate wasteland", whereas Gabriel spoke of starting from "a word to rebuild".

So, by taking a prophecy of destruction, written nineteen years before the destruction actually happened, as a command to rebuild, and then doubling up the figures, we succeed in reaching a seven-year period in which the prophecy was *not* completely fulfilled. Think of it like a race:- By making a false start, and shortening the course, we have reached a point which is not the winning post! I give no prizes for doing that.

Thirdly, Jesus about two hundred years later refers to the abomination of desolation as still future. *(Matt. 24:15.)* So it seems that Antiochus Epiphanes' abomination of desolation was a "mini-fulfilment", almost like a dress rehearsal, or a picture of what is to come—but not a complete fulfilment of the prophecy that Almighty God sent to Daniel through Gabriel.

Fourthly, why did Gabriel bother? Why did Gabriel come down from heaven to tell us about Onias III, of whom I suspect many of my readers will never even have heard? Why did Gabriel come down from heaven to tell us about the jumped-up little tyrant Antiochus Epiphanes? Neither of these was a world-changing figure. But Jesus was.

(b.1) The Messianic (or Traditional) View,
with an ending in 34 A.D.

By this theory, the seven "sevens" and the sixty-two "sevens" (making together sixty-nine "sevens") run their course, and *then,* after the sixty-nine "sevens" (483 years) have ended, an anointed one, a prince, appears. So he is the same person as the anointed one who is cut off. (Contrast the Maccabaean view, in which Cyrus was the anointed prince, but Onias was the anointed one cut off.)

483 years from 458 or 457 B.C. (Artaxerxes' decree in his seventh year which didn't actually specify the rebuilding of Jerusalem, but the people seem to have taken it that way) brings us to 26 or 27 A.D., which some say is the starting year of Jesus' ministry, and so the final "seven" runs from 27 to 34 A.D. At the mid-point of this 7 years, the Messiah stops the sacrifices (or at least brings their practical usefulness to an end) by being cut off (crucified) as the final perfect

sacrifice for all believers. (This theory puts the date of the crucifixion at 30 or 31 A.D.)

So the 490 years ended three and a half years after the crucifixion. What happened at that point of time? Steven, the first Christian martyr, was stoned to death, then Saint Paul (who was present at Steven's stoning) was converted—and he went to preach to the gentiles. He preached *at first* to the Jews, but then to the gentiles—the Jews' 490 years were over: God had finished with them.

This is the "Messianic-but-end-with-Paul" view. There is an alternative "Messianic-but-end-with-Titus" view that we shall look at in a minute.

And so, for us, this view says (just as the Maccabaean view said) that this is all history. It accurately prophesied the coming of our Saviour, but it was all finished by 34 A.D.

A note on punctuation

On the question of whether the seven and the sixty-two should be read together (so the anointed one comes after sixty-nine "sevens", which is what happens in the Messianic view) or whether they should be read separately (so that the anointed one comes after seven "sevens", which is the interpretation under the Maccabaean view) I can only say that the Hebrew as Jesus would have known it has no punctuation. Several centuries later, Hebrew scribes (the Masoretes) added a mark which *may* be to separate the seven and the sixty-two, or *may* be just to emphasise the mystic number seven - or *may* even be to favour the Maccabaean view. In the LXX (the "septuagint", the Greek translation of the Old Testament produced around 250-120 B.C.) the seven and the sixty-two are actually omitted from verse 25. So no final conclusion can be drawn.

The *really* careful reader may have noticed that in my simplified summary of Gabriel's message on page 1 of this book, I combined the seven "sevens" and the sixty-two "sevens" and said, "after sixty-nine sevens"; but in the more academic summary on page 89, I split the seven from the sixty-two and said, "after sixty-two sevens". (But on page 2, I gave a fairly literal rendering of what the words of *Dan. 9:25* actually *say*.)

Problems with the "Messianic-but-end-with-Paul" View

One problem with this view is that awkward final "week". To say that Christ made a seven-year covenant stretching from 27 A.D. to three and a half years after his crucifixion is stretching the wording of the prophecy.

A *second* problem is the assertion that the 490 years began with the decree made by Artaxerxes in his seventh year (458 or 457 B.C.). We took this as an order to rebuild Jerusalem, but *Ezra 4:21* shows us that when Artaxerxes heard that the Jews were rebuilding the walls of Jerusalem, he gave an order, "Stop them! They shall not build unless I give them a command to do so!" So we can hardly be justified in taking his order of 458 or 457 B.C. as an order to build.

We can read about this in *Ezra 4:7-23*, but we need to notice that in ancient times a scribe made a mistake. *Ezra 4:7-23* is in the wrong place. In *Ezra 1:1-4* we can read Cyrus' decree of 538 B.C. ordering the rebuilding of *the Temple*. Work began, but in *Ezra 4:1-6* we see that at the beginning of the reign of Cyrus' successor Ahasuerus (also known as Cambyses: he reigned from 529 to 521 B.C.) enemies of the Jews sent Ahasuerus a letter—and in *Ezra 4:24* (jumping over verses 7-23) we see that the result of this letter was that work on the Temple ceased until the second year of the next king, Darius Hystaspis who reigned from 521 to 485 B.C. In *Ezra 4:7-23*, the ancient scribe has tried to insert the details of the letter to Ahasuerus, but he has inserted the wrong letter. He has inserted the one which Rehum and Shimshai wrote to King Artaxerxes about seventy years later. The correct place for *this* letter would be at the end of the Book of Ezra. If we move it to there, we shall see that the events make sense in date order. Here is what happened:-

The work on the Temple stopped until the second year of Darius Hystaspis, as we have just seen. Then it started again, and the governor Tattenai wrote to Darius about it *(Ezra 5:3)* but Darius ordered a search of the records, found the original decree of Cyrus *(Ezra 6:1-12)* and made an order (in 520 B.C.) that the work was to continue and not be hindered: and the Temple was completed four years later, in 516 B.C., which is seventy years from its destruction in 586 B.C. (Jeremiah said there would be seventy years of desolation, and this is part of the fulfilment of that prophecy—which is why some people argue that Zerubbabel, who undertook the rebuilding, or Joshua who was High Priest at that time, as *Haggai 1:14* tells us, must have been the anointed prince whose coming was prophesied in *Dan. 9:25*.)

Then, more than fifty years after that, King Artaxerxes sent Ezra to Jerusalem with a commission to support the Temple services and enforce the Law of Moses. This was Artaxerxes' decree in the seventh year of his reign (458 or 457 B.C.). Its wording is set out in full in *Ezra 7:11-26*. But if the people took this as a permission to rebuild the city wall, they were mistaken, for Rehum and Shimshai wrote to Artaxerxes. (This is the letter which has been mis-placed into *Ezra 4* when it should be at the end of *Ezra 10*.) The letter is in *Ezra 4:8-16*, and Artaxerxes' answer is in *Ezra 4:17-22* saying, "Make these men stop work, that the city may not be rebuilt until a decree is issued by me"—and in the next verse, *Ezra 4:23*, we see the result: the work was stopped by force. It seems that Rehum and Shimshai and their men actually pulled down much of what had been built, for we find in *Neh. 1:3* "The wall of Jerusalem is broken down and its gates are burnt". When Nehemiah told Artaxerxes of this, Artaxerxes told Nehemiah to go to Jerusalem and rebuild it. *(Neh. 2:1-8.)* This was Artaxerxes' command made in the twentieth year of his reign, 445 or 444 B.C., to rebuild *the city*—but 483 ordinary 365¼ day years from *that* date comes to 39 A.D., several years after Christ's crucifixion, as we shall see on page 96.

But 483 *lunar* years from 445 or 444 B.C. brings us up to 24 or 25 A.D., which is only two years adrift from the year when, according to this theory, Jesus began His ministry. So there's a two-year gap (or maybe not a gap: add seven more lunar years after 24 A.D., and that brings us to 31 A.D. which we saw on page 92 as the alleged date of the crucifixion—except that *that* idea puts the crucifixion at the end of the final "week" instead of in the middle of it).

Thirdly, where is the abomination of desolation? The answer commonly given to that question is that the abomination of desolation was the flock of brazen Roman eagles on the flag-standards of the Roman soldiers on the Temple Mount. So the prince who was to come was the Roman general (and later Emperor) Titus, and the desolation was when his soldiers burnt Jerusalem and the Temple: but that was not until 70 A.D., more than thirty-five years after the end of the 490 years.

That third problem leads us on to the alternative "Messianic" view, the "Messianic-but-end-with-Titus" view.

(b.2) The Messianic (or Traditional) View, but ending with Titus

By this view, the sixty-ninth "seven" ends in 26 or 27 A.D. using the dates we have seen on page 91, or alternatively in 32 or 33 A.D. according to the calculations (running from 445 or 444 B.C.) which we shall see on page 96, but the seventieth "seven" does not then immediately begin. There is a gap. Jesus is crucified, fulfilling the prophecy that *after* the sixty-nine "weeks" Messiah would be cut off: but then ... wait.

The final seven-year "week" is during the period from 66 to 74 A.D. (That actually covers eight years, but call it seven-and-a-bit, or about seven years.) In 66 A.D., the beginning of the final "week", armed rebellion against the Romans broke out in Jerusalem. (The Christians fled from Jerusalem at this time, just before *Luke 21:20-21*—page 11 above—was fulfilled.) Jewish Zealots took over Jerusalem and made the Temple a fortified stronghold. They were fighting for Jewish nationalism and freedom, not for their religion, and they misused and polluted the Temple. In 70 A.D. the Roman legions, led by Emperor Vespasian's son Titus (who subsequently became Emperor, in 79 A.D.) marched in against these rebels. Their Roman banners were an abomination desolating an already-profaned Temple. The Roman soldiers sacked the city and (contrary to Titus' orders) totally destroyed the Temple. That is the mid-point of the final "week". Jews fled, and the rebels made their last stand at the hill-fortress of Masada, which fell in 74 A.D. which is the end of the final "week".

So it's preterism (see page 14). It's all history: it's all over by 74 A.D.

There is another version which puts the finishing-point of the final seven years (its *terminus ad quem* or "terminus to which", as the academics call it) as late as 135 A.D., the date when Emperor Hadrian banished all Jews from Jerusalem. But again, for us, that's all history.

Problems with the "Messianic-but-end-with-Titus" View

First, there is a gap between the end of the sixty-ninth "week" (which was in 26 or 27 A.D. or alternatively 32 or 33 A.D.) and the beginning of the seventieth "week" (66 A.D.). This will be considered in the problems-list on page 100.

Secondly, The second problem set out on page 93 (with King Artaxerxes saying, "Stop them!") applies if we take the seventh year of Artaxerxes (458 or 457 B.C.) as our starting-point (our *terminus a quo* or "terminus *from* which") but not if we take Artaxerxes' twentieth year (445 or 444 B.C.) as our starting-point.

Thirdly, Roman banners as the "abomination of desolation". Not very convincing. (It is much *less* convincing than what Antiochus Epiphanes did.)

So we see that in both the "end-with-Paul" and the "end-with-Titus" versions, the explanation of the final "week" seems ragged and not very convincing.

(c) The End-times (or Futurist) View

This theory starts off in much the same way as the Messianic theory. Sixty-nine "weeks" (483 years) are calculated from the reign of Artaxerxes. In one version, the period is calculated from the decree of Artaxerxes' seventh year, 458 or 457 B.C., so it ends in 26 or 27 A.D., the same as in the Messianic theory. And so it *still* has the problem that Artaxerxes said, "Stop them!" So some people would calculate on the alternative version, 483 *lunar* years from Artaxerxes' twentieth year, 445 or 444 B.C., ending in 24 or 25 A.D., as on page 94 above.

But in a third version (this being the most important one, for the argument put forward in this section) the period is calculated on 360 day Babylonian years from the date of the decree that Artaxerxes in his twentieth year (445 or 444 B.C.) gave to Nehemiah *(Neh. 2:1-8)*. (This is the only one of these decrees that actually orders the rebuilding of Jerusalem, which is what Gabriel's prophecy requires: *Dan. 9:25*.) This is Sir Robert Anderson's theory.

The Anderson theory:- 483 normal 365¼ day years from 445 B.C. would come to 39 A.D. which is several years after the crucifixion, so Anderson's theory uses the ancient Babylonian calendar with its 360 day years, with which Daniel would have been very familiar. 69 x 7 x 360 (i.e. sixty-nine "weeks", each of seven years which are each of 360 days) comes to 173,880 days. Anderson says that as soon as the 173,880 days were complete, Jesus rode on a donkey into Jerusalem as Messiah.

Anderson, confusingly, did his calculation by means of the Julian calendar which was imposed by Julius Caesar, instead of using our present-day Gregorian calendar which was introduced into Europe by Pope Gregory XIII in 1582. The Julian calendar is marginally easier to use for calculations because it has a hundred leap years in four centuries, whereas the Gregorian one has only ninety-seven. So in the seventy "weeks" (490 years) there are 119 leap years on the Julian calendar, but only 116 on the Gregorian one. This is why the Gregorian calendar, which was five days behind the Julian one at the beginning of Anderson's calculation (445 B.C.) was only two days behind it at the end of his calculation (32 A.D.).

There are two other points to note about the calendars. (i) Only the *date* differs between the two calendars. The *day of the week* will always be the same on both calendars. (ii) The Julian calendar *as used in Britain until 1752* had its New Year's Day on March 25th., but that was a local aberration. As imposed by Julius Caesar, it had its New Year's Day on January 1st., even though it retained the old pre-Julian names for the months (so even today we have September, meaning seventh, as our ninth month). So this is a complication we can forget. January 445 B.C. was January 445 B.C. on both calendars. We don't have to jump forwards or backwards a year in the January-to-March period.

For readers who want to spend hours of their valuable time checking the figures for themselves, the **Julian dates are given in bold print** in the following paragraphs, followed by their *Gregorian equivalents in italics*. The word "Gregorian" is abbreviated to "Greg".

Now let us look at Anderson's calculation.

Anderson suggests that Artaxerxes would have made his decree in the first day of the lunar month, as the new moon became visible. Working on data supplied to him by the Astronomer Royal at the Greenwich Royal Observatory (which Anderson set out on page 124 of his book, *The Coming Prince*) Anderson found that the precise moment of new moon in Jerusalem—the moment of potential solar eclipse, when the moon is completely invisible—was 7.09 a.m. on **March 13th., 445 B.C. (Julian)** which was a **Thursday.** *(Thursday, March 8th., 445 B.C. Greg.).* So the next day—the day the new moon became visible—was the first day of the 173,880 days.

According to his book, *The Coming Prince*, this period of 173,880 days runs from **March 14th., 445 B.C. Julian** (which was a **Friday)** *(Friday, March 9th., 445 B.C. Greg.)* to **Sunday, April 6th., 32 A.D. Julian** *(Sunday, April 4th., 32 A.D. Greg.).* So he puts the date of the crucifixion at **Friday, April 11th., 32 A.D. Julian** *(Friday, April 9th., 32 A.D. Greg.).* *(The Coming Prince*, pages 123, 127, 103.)

Unfortunately, Anderson's calculations are three days out! Think of it this way. If you attend *seven* three-day conferences, without a break, they will take exactly three weeks (twenty-one days) so, if they began on a Friday, the last day will be a Thursday. Similarly, if you attend seven eleven-day conferences, they will take exactly eleven weeks, so, if they began on a Friday, *the last day will be a Thursday.* Similarly, if you were able to attend seven (or, for that matter, seventy times seven) 360-day conferences, they would take exactly that number of weeks, so, if they began on a Friday, **the last day will be a Thursday**. Sixty-nine times seven is just like seventy times seven—for it is still *times seven*, and there are seven days in a week. 173,880 days make exactly 24,840 weeks. So if they began on a Friday, *their last day must be a Thursday*.

So Anderson, who puts the start of his 173,880 (69 x 7 x 360) days on **March 14th., 445 B.C. Julian** which was a **Friday** *(Friday, March 9th., 445 B.C. Greg.)* cannot possibly be right in saying that the period ends on **Sunday, April 6th., 32 A.D. Julian** *(Sunday, April 4th., 32 A.D. Greg.)*. His 173,880th day has to be **Thursday, April 3rd., 32 A.D. Julian.** *(Thursday, April 1st., 32 A.D. Greg.)*

Anderson's three-day discrepancy seems to have been caused by confusion over leap years. In his calculation on page 128 of *The Coming Prince*, using the Julian dates of **March 14th., 445 B.C.** and **April 6th., 32 A.D.**, he allows 116 leap years—but by the Julian calendar there had been 119, so from Julian **March 14th., 445 B.C.** to Julian **April 6th., 32 A.D.** had actually been 173,883 days.

The Hoehner theory:- Dr Hoehner of Dallas Theological Seminary has argued in *Bibliotheca Sacra* (see Bibliography) that Anderson's period should start on **March 5th., 444 B.C. Julian**, which was a **Thursday** *(Thursday, Feb. 28th., 444 B.C. Greg.—not Feb. 29th., because the leap year was 445 B.C., not 444 B.C.)* and end on **March 30th., 33 A.D. Julian**, which was a **Monday** *(Monday, March 28th., 33 A.D. Greg.)*. Again we see a discrepancy. Calculating 173,880 days from **Thursday, March 5th., 444 B.C. Julian** *(Thursday, Feb. 28th., 444 B.C. Greg.)* the last day would be on **Wednesday, March 25th., 33 A.D. Julian** *(Wednesday, March 23rd., 33 A.D. Greg.)*. As Hoehner's period of 173,880 days (amounting to exactly 24,840 weeks) begins on a Thursday, its last day *must* therefore be a Wednesday.

Hoehner puts the crucifixion at **Friday, April 3rd., 33 A.D. Julian** *(Friday, April 1st., 33 A.D. Greg.)*.

The year of the crucifixion:- There is much dispute about which year the crucifixion took place. I prefer the 33 A.D. date. Various years have been suggested, but 33 A.D. is the only one in which the Passover full moon was on a Friday. Jesus (our final perfect Passover Sacrifice) was crucified on Good Friday, Passover was observed at full moon (see *Exod. 12:6* in this respect) and the Passover full moon in 33 A.D. was on a Friday. In other years, the Passover full moon was not on a Friday. According to Anderson (page 104 of *The Coming*

Prince—but I have converted his Julian dates to Gregorian) the Gregorian dates of the Paschal (or Passover) full moon were as follows:-

27 A.D. Wednesday, April 7th.	*31 A.D. Tuesday, March 25th.*
28 A.D. Monday, March 27th.	*32 A.D. Monday, April 12th.*
29 A.D. Sunday, April 15th.	*33 A.D. Friday, April 1st.*
30 A.D. Thursday, April 4th.	*34 A.D. Tuesday, March 21st.*

What does all this amount to? We are in danger of not being able to see the wood for the trees here. What we have seen so far in this section is a period of sixty-nine "weeks" or "sevens", which means 173,880 days, running *either* from **Friday, March 14th., 445 B.C.** to **Thursday, April 3rd., 32 A.D.**, *or* from **Thursday, March 5th., 444 B.C.** to **Wednesday, March 25th., 33 A.D.** (all dates Julian—the calendar that Anderson used).   On the other calendar, it means 173,880 days, running *either* from *Friday, March 9th., 445 B.C.* to *Thursday, April 1st., 32 A.D.*, *or* from *Thursday, Feb. 28th., 444 B.C.* to *Wednesday, March 23rd., 33 A.D.* (all dates Gregorian—our modern present-day calendar).

And yet, the discrepancies with regard to these end-dates are of no importance at all. The prophecy is that *after* the end of the 69 "weeks" (the 173,880 days) the Messiah will be cut off. *John 18:28* tells us Christ was crucified at the time of the Passover, which was always celebrated at full moon. How many days after the end of the 173,880 days this was, is immaterial. The point is that the period expired, and then, at the very next Passover, Jesus the Passover Lamb of God was slain, so that on Judgment Day God's terrible judgment will harmlessly pass over those that have trusted in Jesus.

So far, this is the same as the Messianic view. (Yes it is: the only difference is that we have followed a more detailed route to get here!)

But then, read the prophecy carefully.

The rest is future.   After the end of the sixty-nine "weeks" the Messiah will be cut off ... and the people of the prince that shall come will destroy the city and the Temple: and *then* Gabriel describes the final "week". So between the end of the sixty-ninth "week" and the beginning of the seventieth, Gabriel shows that there is a gap, in which the Messiah will be cut off (crucified) and the city and Temple will be destroyed. This destruction happened in 70 A.D. So the 70th "week" should have been from 70 to 77 A.D. (or from 66 to 74 A.D. as in the "end-with-Titus" theory above) unless the gap period extends longer than from 33 to 70 A.D. We know today that it has been *much* longer: it has been the period of nearly 2,000 years which Jesus foresaw as "the times of the gentiles" *(Luke 21:24)* and which is still running today. So the final "week" (of seven 360 day years) is still to come.

By this interpretation, the "people of the coming prince" were the Romans, who destroyed the city and Temple in 70 A.D. The prince—who even today is yet to come—will be the leader of the modern equivalent of the Roman Empire, the EU. This is what we saw on page 4. He will enforce a seven-year covenant or treaty for Israel and Jerusalem—and what happens after that has been considered on pages 4-60 of this book.

Problems with the "futurist" View

First, there is that massive gap between the end of the sixty-ninth "week" and the beginning of the seventieth. (Yes, but Gabriel said there would be a gap. He said that *after* the sixty-ninth "week" the Messiah would be cut off—which happened around 32 or 33 A.D.—and that the people of the prince-to-come would destroy Jerusalem and the Temple—which happened in 70 A.D.—and he, i.e. the EU "prince" who is still to come, would enforce a seven-year covenant or treaty starting the seventieth "week". Jesus in *Luke 21:24* gave the gap a name: "the times of the gentiles". So why didn't Gabriel talk about it in more detail? Well, *why should he?* Why should he talk about the times of the *gentiles* when his prophecy was only concerned with Jerusalem and the *Jews?*)

Second problem: why should Gabriel work on 360 day years? (Be fair to Gabriel: he never once mentions the word "years". He speaks only of "sevens" and does not say sevens of what. But Babylonian 360 day years—albeit with an adjustment every few years—would have been familiar to Daniel.)

Thirdly, this theory applies prophecies given to ancient Israel and Judah (the Jews) to modern Israel. (Yes, but the Jews are the only nation in the history of the world who have been left for nearly two thousand years without a country to call their own, and yet have survived as a recognisable body of people. And now they have a country, in the land of their ancient forefathers. It's called Israel. Israel in the prophecies means Israel. Yet there are people who would apply "replacement theology" at this point and say that what is going to be desolated is not Jerusalem but the Church. We saw on page 45 that the true Church—i.e. all the believers—*will* be desolated: but not because of this prophecy. This prophecy applies to Israel and not to the Church.)

Am I an unfair arguer? On page 90 and again on pages 92 and 95 I outlined three or four problems with the various theories, whereas on page 100 I have outlined three problems and for each of them I have replied with a counter-argument in brackets. Unfair? Let me just say that it would have been unfair of me not to point out that I had done it.

A warning:- The majority of people who accept the end-times interpretation say, "We shall be taken up in the Rapture before the final seven years happens". It is not so. It is not what Scripture says. I fear that many of them will find their faith terribly shaken when they see the events of the final "week" happening in front of their eyes. I hope some of them will read this book and recover their faith as they see what is *really* prophesied.

(d) The "nobody-can-tell" View, and the "schematic" View

There is a fourth school of thought that says we shall *never* solve the numbers-game, and the numbers must be only symbolic. But the problem with that is that a timetable which is not going to be adhered to is pointless. So Gabriel had a wasted journey?

Another idea is that just as the map of London's Underground (with its straight lines and square corners) is not to scale, and yet it is a true *picture* of where the trains go, the "seventy weeks" is not a timescale but is a *picture*—a sketch-plan—of what is to happen. It is *schematic:* it shows the scheme. This is called *chronography*, as against *chronology.*

The warning-flag for the coming of the end of the age

Jesus said in *Matt. 24:36* that no-one knows the time of the end of this age—not even the angels, not even the Son—only the Father. As I write this paragraph, it is still true that no-one knows when it will be. But *Dan. 9:27* tells us that we shall be given seven years' notice of its approach, just as the Jews were given 483 years' notice of the coming of the Messiah, though they could not understand it until the passage of time brought it into focus. In Jesus' day, *some* people realised that the time was at hand. For us, the warning-flag that the time is at hand is Israel's seven-year treaty enforced by peacekeepers from the EU.

A very nasty thought

What if the "time, times and half a time" (which I take to be the final three and a half years of the last "week") are discontinuous, i.e. with gaps like the gap between the sixty-ninth and seventieth "weeks"? It would mean that the final "week" could be spread over many years or even centuries: but I don't think that will happen. I think the final seven years will go through in a continuous seven years.

Conclusion
Take your choice: but my choice is the futurist view.

Daniel 9: what is its source?
Let us end this chapter with some thoughts on where Chapter 9 of the Book of Daniel came from. *Dan. 9:21* tells us that as Daniel was fervently praying, the angel Gabriel appeared! This would have put Daniel under some stress, even though he had met the angel once before (*Dan. 8:16-27*, when Daniel was so terrified, by the vision he saw, that he had to take sick leave). And Gabriel gives him the seventy "weeks" prophecy in *Dan. 9:24-27*. On some of the details, Gabriel is pretty cryptic. For example, in verse 26 he says that the "anointed one" will be cut off וְאֵין לוֹ *v'eyn lo*. Now, my Hebrew is pretty basic, but even I know that *v'eyn lo* means "and there is not to him". But what does "and there is not to him" actually *mean?* Translators have struggled and guessed. "But not for himself" is the Authorised Version; "and shall have nothing" or "and shall have no-one" is in several modern translations, including a Messianic Jewish one. I am not happy with the Jewish Tanakh translation, "the anointed one will disappear and vanish", nor with another Jewish version, "but the kingdom of the Jews will not be his". Other attempts are "although there is nothing against him", "with nothing for himself", "and without sin", "though guiltless", "without a helper", "with no-one to take his part". Knox (translating from the Vulgate *et non erit ejus populus qui eum negaturus est*) says, "the people will disown him and have none of him". Luther has "*und nichts mehr sein*" ("and be no more"). The French is "*et il n'aura pas de successeur*" ("and he will have no heir or successor") and the Italian "*senza che gli resti più nulla*" ("with nothing left to him"). Some commentators assume that a word (such as "justice" or "helpers" or "successors") has been left out, and they try to put it in. Choose your own word? That way, you can choose your own meaning! Let us leave it there and press on.

By the middle of verse 27 (the abomination of desolation) the angel is so angry about the evil thing he is having to predict, that he is spluttering with fury and is no longer talking good Hebrew grammar.

The angel vanishes. Daniel picks up a pen and writes down the prophecy with a shaky hand—shaky partly because of stress and partly because he is more than eighty years old. Academics argue over individual words and the grammar of the word-endings, but some of his writing may have been scarcely legible as he tried to control his shaking hand—assuming that he was writing in Hebrew at all—because Daniel as a government officer was familiar with Babylonian cuneiform script, and so it is quite possible that he wrote (for instance) 𒐐 and 𒐖 instead of שִׁבְעָה and שִׁשִּׁים וּשְׁנַיִם for "seven" and "sixty-two". (No vowel-marks under Daniel's Hebrew: they were not invented until later.) And maybe he wrote out two or three versions, as more details flooded back into his old brain.

> **A note on Babylonian numerals:-** The symbol 𒐕 in Babylonian numerals could stand for one or sixty. When it is placed before 𒐖 (two) it cannot stand for one, so it must be sixty. We have quite a similar rule in English, where a 6 placed before a 2 is read as 60, so 6 2 is sixty-two. Instead of basing calculations on ten or a hundred, as we do, Babylonians based a lot of their astronomical, astrological and mathematical calculations on sixty and six-times-sixty (360) such as 360° in a circle ... and 60° of sky equals two signs of the zodiac ... and they had 360 days in a year (which they had to adjust from time to time because of the seasons, but Gabriel didn't).

Daniel had on previous occasions written records of other events, such as his dream of four empires *(Dan. 7)* and his previous encounter with the angel. And somebody somewhere had recorded the fact that Daniel had once been thrown to the lions and had had a miraculous escape. Then, after Daniel's death, some devout person pinned these pieces of parchment and papyrus together, and there we have the beginnings of the Book of Daniel.

More than three hundred years later, someone living under the persecution which Antiochus Epiphanes imposed on the Jews, thought, "These prophecies apply to today!" and added various bits and details (including perhaps the pretty accurate historical account in *Dan. 11:5-35* of the fighting which had taken place between the kings of the south, i.e. the Egyptian Ptolemies, and the kings of the north, i.e. the Greek and Syrian Seleucids, down to the time of the present oppressor Antiochus Epiphanes) and made it a rallying-call for resistance. (I say this only as a possible opinion, not as a proven fact.)

In this form, the book was accepted into the Hebrew scriptures, but only as part of the "writings", not as part of the "books of the prophets".

(This is why, in Jewish editions of the Old Testament, the Book of Daniel, with one or two other books, is pushed to the end of the Old Testament.) The LXX, the "septuagint" Greek translation of the Hebrew scriptures (called "septuagint" which means "seventy" because it is said to have had about seventy translators, and in which the translation of the Book of Daniel was probably made about 150 B.C.) seems to have been made by translators who believed that *Dan. 9* was a prophecy about the times of Antiochus Epiphanes. It handles *Dan. 9:24-27* so badly that it is not a translation—it is not even a paraphrase—it is like a commentary, saying what *they* believed. But the Jews in Israel still used the Hebrew version. This is the version Jesus would have known.

The Hebrew was written in consonantal text (so, for instance, the word "consonantal" would be spelt "cnsnntl") but people knew how to pronounce it. More than five hundred years later, when the Jews were scattered and very few could speak Hebrew, the Masoretic scribes added vowels. The result is the Masoretic text, the version of the Hebrew scriptures which we have today. The oldest surviving copy of the Masoretic text is one made in 925 A.D. Until the mid-twentieth century, scholars assumed that over the centuries, as copies of copies were made, errors and omissions by scribes would have resulted in lots of mistakes in the text. So, if a hard-to-make-sense-of passage was encountered, it was easy to assume that the problem was due to bad copying. Then the Dead Sea scrolls were discovered, containing Old Testament texts (including eight fragments of the Book of Daniel) which were eight hundred or in some cases even a thousand years older than any which had previously been available, and scholars were astonished to see how little had changed in the text in a thousand years.

But adding vowels can be a matter of opinion. On page 50 of Dr Hoehner's article on the seventy "weeks" there is a misprint: the word "thre" appears. An "e" has been left out, so put it in. But should the word be "there" or should it be "three"? It makes a difference!

And most of us do not speak fluent Hebrew, and have to rely on translations—and the variety of the translations shows that the translators have had trouble working out the exact meaning of the text, particularly in *Dan. 9:27*, where either the angel was too angry to speak clearly, or Daniel was too shaky to write it clearly—or both.

But in this mangled mixture we still have a sufficient (though imperfect) record of God's prophecy which he sent through Gabriel: and God's prophecy will be fulfilled.

- - - - -

Chapter 12

Peter: a focus far further afield

In *2 Peter 3:10-13* we find it written:

> The day of the Lord will come like a thief, in which the heavens will pass away with a roar and the elements will be destroyed with intense heat, and the earth and its works will be burnt up. ... the heavens will be destroyed by burning, and the elements will melt with intense heat. But according to his promise we are looking for new heavens and a new earth, in which righteousness dwells.

This seems to be parallel to *Rev. 20:7-11* and *21:1*,

> When the thousand years are completed, Satan will be released from his prison, and will come out to deceive the nations which are in the four corners of the earth, Gog and Magog, to gather them together for the war ... and fire came down from heaven and devoured them. ... And I saw a great white throne and him who sat on it, from whose presence earth and heaven fled away ... and I saw a new heaven and a new earth, for the first heaven and the first earth passed away, and there was no longer any sea.

That's the end of the world—the *end* of the millennium—the *end* of the thousand years of peace. It's still more than a thousand years away.

The Qur'an also has this prophecy—though the reservation I expressed at the end of chapter 10 applies equally to these verses:

> Do you not see that Allah created the heavens and the earth in Truth? If He so wishes, He can remove you and put (in your place) a **new Creation**. For Allah that is no great matter. *(Sura 14:19-20.)*

> Say: "Travel through the earth and see how Allah did originate creation; so will Allah produce a **later creation**: for Allah has power over all things". *(Sura 29:20.)*

Look at *Is. 65:17* "Behold, I will create new heavens and a new earth: and the former things shall not be remembered nor come to mind." Here is *Genesis 1:2* all over again. A new Creation.

If anything at all was not burnt to powder in that fiery destruction, perhaps the inhabitants of that new earth will puzzle over the fossil of a fragment of a cow in much the same way that we gaze in perplexity at the fossilised bone of a dinosaur! Here is an account of *Gen. 1:1-31 (etc.)* which is *very* highly speculative, and if it upsets creationists and evolutionists *equally*—well that's equality, isn't it?

Creation

Note: words of scripture are in normal print: comments and explanations are in italics.

Gen. 1:1   In the beginning God *(so God existed before the beginning. God is eternal—and infinite.)*
In the beginning *(perhaps 15 thousand million years ago)* God **created** *(Big Bang)* the heavens and the earth.
(The earth was a wonderful place with "carboniferous" forests of trees with leaves like ferns. And then, about 250 million years ago, a comet or an asteroid smashed into the earth. Everything died, and there were great upheavals which pushed up new mountain ranges and buried the forests, so the trees eventually turned into coal: and that was the end of the age that geologists call the Palaeozoic Age.)

Gen. 1:2   And the earth was formless and void (or waste and empty) and darkness was over the surface of the deep.
(Then, perhaps 75 million years later) The Spirit of God was moving over the surface of the waters.

Gen. 1:3   Then God said, "Let there be light" and *(the clouds became thinner and)* there was light.   *(Remember: the heavens already existed: Gen. 1:1.)*
(And the earth was a wonderful place, with dinosaurs trotting around in it. And then, about 75 million years ago, a comet or an asteroid smashed into the earth. Scientists know where it hit: it was near Chixculub at the northern end of the Yucatan Peninsula in Mexico in Central America, and it hit with such force that—according to one theory—it caused a bulge of mountains, known today as the Deccan Traps, in India, on the far side of the planet. That was the end of the dinosaurs, and the end of the age that geologists call the Mesozioc Age.)

Gen. 1:2   And the earth was waste *(again)* and empty, and darkness was over the surface of the deep.
(Then, perhaps 75 million years later) The Spirit of God was moving over the surface of the waters.

Gen. 1:3	Then God said, "Let there be light" and *(the clouds became thinner and)* there was light.
Gen. 1:4	God called the light "day" and the darkness "night".
Gen. 1:5	And there was evening and morning: the first day.
Gen. 1:6-8	God made an expanse called "sky" which separated the waters above it from the waters below it. *(Earth was in the centre of a bubble!)* This was the second day.
Gen. 1:9-13	Dry land, and vegetation. The third day.
Gen. 1:14-15	God said, "Let there be lights in the sky".
Gen. 1:16-19	God made two great lights, and also the stars. The fourth day. *(The Bible says God <u>made</u> the lights. It does not say <u>created</u>. Is this where they shine through and become visible? Could it be that they—or the material they are made of—had existed ever since Gen. 1:1?)*
Gen. 1:20	Let the water teem with living creatures, and let birds fly.
Gen. 1:21-23	So God **created** the great sea creatures, and birds. The fifth day.
Gen. 1:24	And God said, "Let the land produce animals".
Gen. 1:25	God made the animals. *(The word "created"—i.e. made out of nothing—is only used three times in Gen. 1. It is used in Gen. 1:1 for creation of matter; in Gen. 1:21 for creation of the first living creatures, and in Gen. 1:27 for the creation of man. Everything else was "made".)*
Gen. 1:26	God said, "Let us make man".
Gen. 1:27-31	God **created** man. The sixth day.
Gen. 2:1-2	God rested the seventh day. *(At this time, the earth had a canopy of water above the sky, as we saw in Gen. 1:6-8 above.)*
Gen. 3	The Fall: loss of the Garden of Eden *(which was on the River Euphrates, according to Gen. 2:14, so it was probably in Iraq).*
Gen. 4 - 5	Cain, Abel, Seth, and further generations down to Noah.
Gen. 6 - 8	The flood. *(So the water-canopy came crashing down and flooded the whole earth. When all this water ran off into the sea as the flood receded, it would have made the sea deeper. This may have been the time*

when Britain became an island, separated from France by water. Before then, the continental shelf, west of Ireland, may have been the old coastline. This would have been the time when the earth's geography took on the shape that we know today.)

Then we get Abraham, Isaac, Jacob ... Moses ... David, Solomon ... the Old Testament prophets ... Jesus ... the Church, and us today. Then:-

Rev. 8:8   Something like a huge mountain, all ablaze, was thrown into the sea.

Rev. 8:10   A great star, blazing like a torch, fell from the sky.

Rev. 16:16-20   They gathered the kings together to Armageddon. ... And a severe earthquake took place. No earthquake like it has ever occurred since humanity has been on the earth, so tremendous was the quake. ... Every island fled away and the mountains could not be found. *(If these verses from Rev. 8 and Rev. 16 are a description of a comet or asteroid, breaking up and crashing into the earth, it causes immense damage, but it does not leave the earth "void".)*

Isaiah 24:1, 6 and 19   The Lord lays the earth waste, devastates it, distorts its surface, and scatters its inhabitants. ... The inhabitants of the earth are burned, and few are left. ... The earth is broken asunder, split through, shaken violently...

Rev. 19:11   Jesus returns.

Rev. 20:1-6   The millennium.

Rev. 20:7-15   The end of the millennium, and the Last Judgment.

2 Peter 3:7   The present heavens and earth are being reserved for fire, kept for the Day of Judgment. *(It is not clear whether "heavens" here means the sky or the entire universe.)*

2 Peter 3:10   The heavens will pass away with a roar and the elements will be destroyed with intense heat, and the earth and its works will be burnt up (or, according to some manuscripts, will be laid bare). *(Then the earth will be void!) Let the fire cool down, for millions of years. Then, perhaps 75 million years later, when the earth is cooler but is waste and void:-*

Joel and various	Islam	Asteroid Theory	Revelation	Daniel (timescale)
	The Mahdi (a messiah) will come		1st seal: white horse: emergence of a great leader	
re-incarnation of Vishnu? Bhagavad-Gita IV, 5-8				Treaty enforced by peacekeepers sent by EU leader keeps Jewish and Palestinian extremists apart (start of final seven years)
general ecology: global warming			*To unbelievers:- THE CHALLENGE OF GOG. Believe what you read in this book when you see Israel's northern invader destroyed by fire from heaven.*	1 year

Ezekiel

Joel and various	Islam	Asteroid Theory	Revelation	Ezekiel	Daniel (timescale)
Joel's 1st swarm of "locusts"	"Gog & Magog" swarm down from the north after the return of Jesus, but are destroyed in a single night by insects or worms biting their necks, and they will stink.	asteroid's near-miss showers meteorites onto the invaders *(Jews see this as a miracle and immediately rebuild the Temple)*	2nd seal: red horse signifying war	Israel is invaded by "Gog" from the north: but the invading army is destroyed in a single day by fire from heaven. 7 months is needed to bury the dead. And they stink.	2 years
Who stopped the sacrifices? Antiochus? or Jesus? or the antichrist?	The Dajjal (the antichrist) will come, but cannot enter the city of Medina.	asteroid now showers more meteorites & larger bolides	1st trumpet, 3rd seal, 2nd & 3rd trumpets, 4th seal, 4th & 5th trumpets, 5th seal, image of the beast (abomination of desolation) erected in the Jerusalem Temple. Jews flee. The Jews are persecuted but are protected in the desert. 666 economics system, Christians persecuted.	**Matt., Mk.** abomination of desolation in the Temple in Jerusalem	3 years 3½ erection of abomination of desolation 4 years

A T I M E   —   Joel's 2nd swarm of "locusts"?

Diagram 12 of 12

G R E A T   T R I B U L A T I O N

Joel and various	Islam	Asteroid Theory	Revelation	Daniel (timescale)
T I M E S & Joel's 3rd swarm of "locusts"? Is. 34:4	The sun will rise from the west: a trumpet shall sound: the stars become dim, the moon dark and rent apart, the mountains are removed, and the heavens roll up like a scroll.	another bolide	6th trumpet: 200 million invaders are preparing to advance from the far east.	5 years
H A L F sky rolled like a scroll Rev. 14:15 earth harvested.	Jesus will kill the Dajjal, Allah will defeat the Jews. A time of plenty will come but then all good people will die & the End comes.	further onslaught from the asteroid; devastation; the greatest earthquake ever as it finally crashes into the planet.	6th seal: earthquake, sky rolled like a scroll, sun dark, stars fall: 7th trumpet & the rapture.	**Luke** signs in sun, moon and stars — sun and moon dark, stars fall, angels gather the elect 6 yrs **Paul** rapture at the last trumpet
A T I M E Joel's 4th swarm of "locusts", all nations against Jerusalem.			Then 7th seal with 7 bowls of divine wrath, but in heaven the marriage-supper of the Lamb. Then Jesus returns in glory; Armageddon; Satan is bound and the millennium (1,000 years of peace) begins.	Dan. 12:7 Is it 164 B.C.? 34 or 74 A.D.? 7 yrs. future? Armageddon

Gen. 1:2   The Spirit of God was moving over the surface of the planet. *(The reason I have altered "waters" to "planet" is because Rev. 21:1 below says that there is no more sea.)*

Gen. 1:3   Then God said, "Let there be light" and *(the clouds became thinner and)* there was light.

2 Peter 3:13   According to His promise we are looking for new heavens and a new earth, in which righteousness dwells.

Isaiah 65:17   I create new heavens and a new earth; and the former things shall not be remembered or come to mind.

Rev. 21:1   Then I saw a new heaven and a new earth, for the first heaven and the first earth had passed away, and there was no more sea.

Try to imagine a scientist on that new earth **about six thousand years later,** *and he discovers a fossilised fragment of a cow which had not been completely burnt up. And a creationist tells him,*

"It cannot be ancient, because the Creation was only six thousand years ago!"

And then just at that moment an evolutionist comes along and joins in the discussion and tells them,

"It is 75 million years old, which proves that the story that the Creation was only six thousand years ago is a myth, and we all developed by evolution!"

Who is right?

Rev. 21:2   I saw the holy city, the new Jerusalem, coming down out of heaven from God.

Rev. 21:23   The city does not need the sun or the moon to shine on it, for the glory of God gives it light, and the Lamb is its lamp.

Eph. 3:21 (AV) World without end, Amen.

- - - - -

Chapter 13

What shall we do?

In 1970, when I was a young Christian, less knowledgeable but more alive than I am now, I wrote a ten-page booklet called *How do I become a Christian?* I had a thousand copies printed, and handed them out to all and sundry.

Thirty-seven years later, I cannot improve on it, so here it is:-

3.

Life after Death

When we die, our souls go either to heaven, where God gives us everlasting life with Him, or to hell, the place of everlasting death.

. **THE BIBLE SAYS** "The soul that sins, it shall die" (Ezekiel **18,20**).

Nothing we can do will solve the problem.

I'VE ONLY DONE A FEW BAD THINGS! WON'T ALL THE GOOD THINGS I'VE DONE COUNT AGAINST THEM & MAKE ME ALRIGHT?

IF YOU WERE STOPPED FOR CARELESS DRIVING, WOULD YOU EXPECT THE TIMES YOU HAD DRIVEN WELL TO COUNT AGAINST THE TIME YOU HAD DRIVEN BADLY? YOU WOULD STILL BE FOUND GUILTY!

'I'M SORRY!

2.

A Christian believes in Jesus Christ.

And a Christian believes that Jesus is **God's** answer to **Man's Biggest Problem.**

My biggest problem is my bad self.
The Bible says we all have this problem. Some have it more than others but there is no difference, we have all got it. — So we all do things that are wrong.
The Bible calls these things **SIN**

THE BIBLE SAYS "All have sinned & come short of the glory of God."
(Romans **3, 23**)

NOBODY IS PERFECT!
SIN = all the things that stop us being perfect & make us what we are.

It's like this:-

(from our Crime Reporter)

5.

Drama in Court
Judge pays Prisoner's Penalty

Lord Chief Justice Fairlove, sitting in the Supreme Court of the State of Titipu today, imposed a severe fine. "Friend or not, I will not find a guilty man innocent," he stated. "Justice must be done and will be done."

Knowing however that the defendant was not able to pay the amount of the fine, the Judge offered to pay it for him. As the Court officers were leading the defendant away to the cells he accepted the Judge's offer and expressed grateful thanks. As soon as the fine had been paid the officers released the defendant, who left the Court, in a state of some amazement, a free man.

Prisoner Released!

That is what Jesus has done for us:-

The penalty for sin is death, and Jesus has paid our penalty, if we accept his offer of free forgiveness.

4.

The Problem Solved:-

The Bible tells us the answer.

The solution to the problem is not anything we can do. It is something God has done.

THE BIBLE SAYS "Christ Jesus came into the world to save sinners." (1 Timothy 1.15)

JESUS

Born at Bethlehem. God in human form. The only man who has ever lived a sinless life. Died in agony after men nailed him on a cross. AROSE FROM THE DEAD & many people saw him. Did not die again, but ascended into Heaven and is alive today.

THE BIBLE SAYS "God loved the world so much that He gave His only Son, so that whoever believes in him should not perish but have everlasting life." (John 3.16.)

7.

What must I do?

Accept God's free gift: believe in Jesus Christ to forgive your sins & to make a difference to your life.

Don't believe in

the government ✗

your own good deeds ✗

the Church ✗

Believe in Jesus Christ. ✓

That is how to become a Christian.

THE BIBLE SAYS "Believe in the Lord Jesus & you will be saved." (Acts 16.31.)

DOES IT COST ANYTHING?

1. You will have to be willing to give up your sins & to obey God.
2. Some people are sure to laugh at you, & may possibly do worse than that.

6.

What happens if I become a Christian?

Two things:-

1. God forgives all your sins because they are all put on Jesus.

2. God's Holy Spirit will find himself a place in your innermost being, & will give you power to give up your sins & live the way God wants.

(It is most unlikely that you will completely give up your sins at once, but you can expect to become better, because when you become a Christian you give God a claim on your whole life, & He has the right to do things with it.)

9.

HINTS for Young CHRISTIANS

1.) When you become a Christian you may not feel any different, but this is not important. Think about the FACTS. not your feelings.

2.) You will gain joy and strength from talking to God in prayer. Make it regular, daily.

3.) By reading God's Word the Bible you will learn more about Him.

4.) Being in contact with other Christians will help you, so join a Church. (But if you belong to one of those Churches which do not have a regular Prayer Meeting or Bible Study Group, you might do well to change

[CONTINUED OVERLEAF→]

8.

A Prayer

(What you say in words is not of the greatest importance. It is what you believe in your heart that is vital. But if in your heart you believe on Christ it will probably help you to pray this prayer.)

"O God, I ADMIT that I have done wrong. I AM SORRY and I want to turn away from my wrongs for ever. I BELIEVE Jesus Christ died to pay the penalty for all my wrongs. and I OPEN MY HEART TO HIM so that He can cleanse me and lead me in a new life, in which I can resist temptation in the power which your Holy Spirit gives. Thankyou, Lord. Amen."

10.

to one which does.)

5.) The devil will still catch you off guard & make you sin sometimes. Try to avoid this, but when it happens tell God you are sorry, rely on Christ for forgiveness, & go on being a Christian.

   In the Bible there is a passage (1 John 1, 8-9) which was written to people who had been Christians for years: which says, "If we say that we have no sin, we deceive ourselves & the truth is not in us. If we confess our sins He is faithful & just to forgive us our sins & to cleanse us from all unrighteousness."

                    +

"Believe in the Lord Jesus and you shall be saved." *(Acts 16:31.)*

- - - - - - -

Further copies of this book may be obtained direct from the author at 92, Hillside Road, Portishead, Bristol BS20 8LJ, for £4.00 (January 2007 price) plus 50p. towards postage, or post-free if two or more copies are ordered. (Buy now for Christmas!) Please state your address and postcode clearly. Cheques with order, please, in favour of the author, John A. Greed.

APPENDIX 1: the Matthew-Mark-Luke comparison referred to on page 12.

Matt. 10:5-22. SENDING TWELVE	*Mk. 13:8-14.*	*Luke 9:1-10.* SENDING TWELVE
<u>A</u> These twelve Jesus sent out after instructing them. ...	OLIVET DISCOURSE	<u>A</u> And He called the twelve together ... and He sent them out.

Whoever does not receive you ... <u>B</u> shake off the dust of your feet. ... I send you out <u>C</u> as sheep in the midst of wolves; therefore be shrewd as serpents, and innocent as doves. But beware of men; for <u>D</u> they will deliver you up to the courts, and <u>E</u> scourge you in their synagogues; and <u>F</u> you shall even be brought before governors and kings for My sake, as <u>G</u> a testimony to them and to the Gentiles. But when they deliver you up, <u>H</u> do not become anxious about how or what you will speak; for it shall be given you in that hour what you are to speak. For it is not you who speak, but <u>I</u> it is the Spirit of your Father who speaks in you. And <u>J</u> brother will deliver up brother <u>K</u> to death, and a father his child; and children will rise up against parents, and cause them to be <u>K</u> put to death. And <u>L</u> you will be hated by all on account of My name, but <u>M</u> it is the one who has endured to the end who will be saved.

Matt. 24:7-15. OLIVET DISCOURSE

<u>N</u> ... famines and earthquakes ... merely the beginning of birth pangs. Then they <u>D</u> will deliver you up to tribulation, and <u>K</u> will kill you, and <u>L</u> you will be hated by all nations on account of My name. And at that time many will fall away and will betray one another and hate one another. And many false prophets will arise, and will mislead many. And because lawlessness is increased, most people's love will grow cold. But <u>M</u> the one who endures to the end, it is that one who shall be saved. And this gospel of the kingdom shall be <u>O</u> preached in the whole world for a witness to all the nations, and then the end shall come. Therefore <u>P</u> when you see the abomination of desolation ...

<u>N</u> ... earthquakes ... famines ... merely the beginning of birth pangs. But be on your guard; for <u>D</u> they will deliver you up to the courts, and <u>E</u> you will be flogged in the synagogues, and <u>F</u> you will stand before governors and kings for My sake, as <u>G</u> a testimony to them. And the gospel must first be <u>O</u> preached to all the nations. And when they arrest you and deliver you up, <u>H</u> do not be anxious beforehand about what you are to say, but say whatever is given you in that hour; for it is not you who speak, but <u>I</u> it is the Holy Spirit. And <u>J</u> brother will deliver up brother <u>K</u> to death, and a father his child; and children will rise up against parents and cause them to be <u>K</u> put to death. And <u>L</u> you will be hated by all on account of My name, but <u>M</u> it is the one who has endured to the end who will be saved. But <u>P</u> when you see the abomination of desolation ...

As for those who do not receive you, ... <u>B</u> shake off the dust from your feet as a testimony against them.

And when the apostles returned, they gave an account to Him of all that they had done.

Luke 10:1-11. SENDING SEVENTY

The Lord appointed seventy others, and sent them two and two ahead of Him.

I send you out <u>C</u> as lambs in the midst of wolves. ... Whatever city you enter and they do not receive you, ... say, <u>B</u> "Even the dust of your city which clings to our feet, we wipe off..."

Luke 21:11-20. OLIVET DISCOURSE

<u>N</u> ... earthquakes ... plagues and famines ... terrors and great signs from heaven. But before all these things, they will lay their hands on you and will persecute you, <u>E</u>, <u>D</u> delivering you to the synagogues and prisons, <u>F</u> bringing you before kings and governors for My name's sake. It will lead to an opportunity for <u>G</u> your testimony. So <u>H</u> make up your minds not to prepare beforehand to defend yourselves; for <u>I</u> I will give you utterance and wisdom which none of your opponents will be able to resist or refute. But <u>J</u> you will be betrayed even by parents and brothers and relatives and friends, and they will <u>K</u> put some of you to death, and <u>L</u> you will be hated by all on account of My name. Yet not a hair of your head will perish. By your <u>M</u> perseverance you will win your souls. But when you see Jerusalem surrounded by armies ...

APPENDIX 2: Nebuchadnezzar's boast. Extracts from the Babylonian "cylinders" referred to on page 89.

On pages 19-23 of his *Babylonian Life and History*, E. A. Wallis Budge (an assistant in the Department of Oriental Antiquities at the British Museum) gives a long account of a translation of two Babylonian cylinders which were acquired by the British Museum in 1878. Unfortunately he does not give the Museum's reference-numbers for them.[1] Extracts from his account are set out below.

This appendix is printed as shown in Budge's book, except that in five places I have added explanations *in italics in square brackets*.

Column I
1.   Nebuchadnezzar the King of Babylon,
2.   the exalted prince, the worshipper of the god Marduk,
3.   the supreme lord, the beloved of the god Nebo...

15.   I put my trust in Marduk, my lord, my judge,
16.   his supreme fortress, the citadel the high place, [the walls]
17.   Imgur-Bel, Nimitti-Bel, *[these were the two city walls]*
18.   I caused to be completed over against [their] great fortresses.
19.   Upon the threshold of its great gates,
20.   mighty lords (gods)
21.   and [images] of poisonous snakes
22.   I set up,
23.   the which never had any king *[who was]* my predecessor made.
24.   The quay (of the fortress), its ditch (moat),
25.   with bitumen and brick
26.   the father, my begetter, built and completed for a bulwark(?).
27.   As for me, the paths of the ancient quay
28.   once, twice *[i.e. two courses of brickwork]*
29.   I built up with bitumen and brick, and
30.   the quay which my father had worked at I excavated.
31.   I caused its foundations to be laid with huge flat slabs, and
32.   I raised up its summit like a mountain.
33.   The quay of brick at the ford of the setting sun
34.   within Babylon I completed. ...
      [This quay would be a landing-place on the Euphrates.]

Column II
13.   Four thousand cubits square, the citadel with walls
14.   towering and inaccessible,
15.   the everlasting fortress of Babylon at the ford of the rising sun,
16.   I caused to surround.
17.   I dug out the moat, I emptied away the water that had gathered there,
18.   I made its bed of bitumen and brick, and I excavated
19.   the quay which my father had worked at,
20.   the lofty fortress with bitumen and brick
21.   I built up like a mountain upon its sides.
22.   The height of the fortress of Borsippa thoroughly
23.   I rebuilt.
24.   The quay and the moat [lined and built] with bitumen and brick
25.   I made to surround the citadel for a protection.
26.   For the god Turkit, the lord, the breaker of the weapons of my enemies
27.   I rebuilt his temple within Borsippa. ...
       [Borsippa is about eight or nine miles, or about fifteen kilometres, from Babylon.]

44.   An account of all my magnificent works
45.   and of my restorations of the temples of the great gods
46.   above what the kings my fathers wrote
47.   upon a stone tablet I wrote; and
48.   I set it up for future days.

- - - - -

Gabriel is fully aware of Nebuchadnezzar's boast, and I suggest he is saying to Daniel that Jerusalem will be rebuilt, just like that.

---

1   The British Museum has given me the reference-numbers ANE 91131 - 91133 and Rm 674 in the Museum's Department of the Ancient Near East, for these cylinders.

Bibliography

Anderson, Sir R.   *The Coming Prince*   (Grand Rapids, Michigan: Kregel
19th. edn, 1975   Publications. ISBN 0-8254-2115-2).

Budge, E. A. W.   *Babylonian Life and History* (London: The Religious Tract Society).
3rd. edn, 1891

al-Bukhari   *Sahih Al-Bukhari* Vols 1-9 (Beirut: Dar al Arabia) translated by
1985 edn   Dr. Muhammad Muhsin Khan, Islamic University, Al-Medina,
             Al-Munauwara.

al-Bukhari   *Summarised Sahih Al-Bukhari* (Riyadh: Maktaba Dar-us-Salam)
1994 edn   translated by Dr. Muhammad Muhsin Khan.

abu Dawud   *Sunan Abu Dawud* Vols 1-3 (Lahore: SH Muhammad Ashraf.
1996 reprint   ISBNs 969-432-096-8, 969-432-097-6 and 969-432-098-4) translated
             by Prof. Ahmad Hasan, Islamabad.

Hoehner, H. W.   "Chronological Aspects of the Life of Christ, Part VI: Daniel's Seventy
1975   Weeks and New Testament Chronology" in Zuck, R. B. (ed.)
         Bibliotheca Sacra Vol. 132 (Dallas, Texas: Dallas Theological
         Seminary. ISSN 0006-1921) 47-65.

Josephus, F.   *The Works of Flavius Josephus* (London and Edinburgh: William P.
             Nimmo) translated by Professor William Whiston, Cambridge.

ibn Kathir   *The Signs before the Day of Judgement* (London: Dar Al Taqwa
1991 translation   Ltd. ISBN 1-870582-03-9) translated by Mrs. Huda Khattab.
2000 reprint

Levy, David H.   *Comets: Creators and Destroyers* (New York: Touchstone, a
1998   trademark of Simon & Schuster Inc. ISBN 0-684-85255-1).

Imam Muslim   *Sahih Muslim* Vols 1-4 (Pakistan: publisher's name & address not
1974 translation   stated) translated by 'Abdul Hamid Siddiqi.

Peebles, A. C.   *Asteroids: a History* (Washington and London: Smithsonian
2000   Institution Press. ISBN 1-56098-389-2).
         Pages 195-204 of this book give a good scientific account of the
         impact of the comet Shoemaker Levy 9 into Jupiter.

Wallis Budge   *see* Budge.

Zuck, R. B. (ed.)   *see* Hoehner.

- - - - -